BORDERLINE PERSONALITY DISORDER

SURVIVAL GUIDE

FROM CHAOS TO AUTHENTICITY

OTHER BOOKS BY MARK S. SILVER

<u>FORENSICS</u>

Psychosocial Evaluations and Consultation in Civil Litigation:
Strategies to Understand and Humanize the Client (2021)

Handbook of Mitigation in Criminal and Immigration Forensics:
Humanizing the Client Towards a Better Legal Outcome,
Seventh Edition (2021)

Criminal Mitigation Case Studies for Criminal Defense Lawyers:
Strategies for Pre-Plea and Pre-Sentencing (2017)

Forensic Social Work Case Studies: Personal Injury, Family,
Immigration, and Criminal Mitigation Consulting (2018)

<u>NOVELS</u>

The Arranged Marriage: My Kalpa (2016)

Res Ipsa Loquitor: The Mystery of the Dead Dean (2017)

<u>SHORT FICTION</u>

Extreme Hardship: An Asian Journey. Kindle Edition (2010)

BORDERLINE PERSONALITY DISORDER

SURVIVAL GUIDE

FROM CHAOS TO AUTHENTICITY

MARK S. SILVER

atmosphere press

Published by Atmosphere Press
Atmospherepress.com

ISBN 979-8-89132-120-5

Cover design by Dhiraj Navlakhe

First Edition. January 2024.

For further information, visit www.MARKSSILVER.com
or contact Mark Silver at: MarkSilver1@cs.com

To: Friends

In 1992 my father, Dr. Daniel Silver, published the co-edited book
Handbook of Borderline Disorders.

Although I have dedicated other books to my father,
I am grateful to include him as an important inspiration of
humanistic psychiatric practice.

I know my heart, and have studied mankind; I am not made like any one I have been acquainted with, perhaps like no one in existence; if not better, I at least claim originality, and whether Nature did wisely in breaking the mold with which she formed me, can only be determined after having read this work.

—Jean-Jacques Rousseau, *Confessions*, Book I

TABLE OF CONTENTS

Get a Dog (But Only One)

Reconsider Reproducing

Choose Someone Who Can Tolerate You

Consider the Road Less Traveled

Don't Leave the Movie Early

Keep Your Sense of Humor

Almost No One Will Understand You

Mirror Staring

Eating Healthy is Not a Panacea Nor is Exercise

External Security Permits Internal Control

Listen, Look, and Learn

Make It a Habit to Be Inspired

Financial Independence is Priceless

Volunteer to Help Others in Need

PART I

CHAPTER 1

Introduction: Chaos

Audience

> Courage is not having the strength to go on; it is going on when you don't have the strength.
> - Teddy Roosevelt

This book is written for people who suffer with Borderline Personality Disorder (BPD) and those who wish to understand BPD (most likely because they have a family member with the disorder). Additionally, many people will hopefully be able to identify with and benefit from different aspects of this book even if they do not meet the criteria of BPD. People who act in self-destructive ways, for example, will hopefully benefit from those parts of the book that focus on self-destructive behavior.

Purpose

> Algernon: The doctors found out that Bunbury could not live... so Bunbury died.
>
> Lady Bracknell: He seems to have had great confidence in the opinion of his physicians.
> - Oscar Wilde, *The Importance of Being Earnest*

This book is not a clinical text, but a survival guide. Clinical experts are welcome to read the book—Lord knows I want to sell as many books as possible—but the goal of the book is to assist the borderline to live a more content, safe, stable, authentic, coherent, and healthy life by considering a broader understanding of BPD and specific survival strategies to ensure that the borderline and family members do not ignore important warning signs (or miss opportunities to intervene). A survival guide is needed because BPD causes profound harm, including inner emptiness, sadness, anxiety, confusion, impulsivity, emotional lability, and feelings of terrible loneliness, robbing the person of his personal dignity.

When a borderline feels damaged he is feeling the cumulative product of genetic (nature) and environmental (nurture) influences. Our genetics are set, our caregivers are set (as were their genetics and caregivers), our environment is set, we have few if any choices about which schools to attend, our socialization is primarily set, and even our religious beliefs and value system may be set due to cultural mores and traditions. There is a corollary to this crucial for parents to understand. We can do relatively little for our children because so much is indeed set in their lives. Parent's protect children from physical and emotional harm and trauma that the child's developing consciousness cannot anticipate or comprehend. The healthy and mature parent entices the child to fall in love with learning (curiosity) and life (exploration), which may even yield positive epigenetic changes, in a safe home with unconditional love—and act as good role models so that the child can grow up enjoying proper regard for self and other with appropriate love, trust, and good judgment.

Thus, our ability to control our childhood experiences or environment is quite limited and by the time we do have control of our lives in early adulthood, we have already been directed to behave, feel, and think in a circumscribed manner. At some point, we need to take control of our lives maturely and thoughtfully and this is even more true for the borderline who has felt helpless or unable to change his experience or environment. *This book will hopefully help the borderline to understand and control behavior, emotion, and thinking to live a more meaningful and dignified life. My most important conclusion is that life-skills development and maintaining a healthy lifestyle—as trite as that may sound—can yield the greatest happiness, even for those suffering with profound psychological pain.*

High-Functioning and Low-Functioning

I'm a very needy person and I'm deeply insecure.
   – *White Lotus*, S2:E5

I have written this book for both the high-functioning and low-functioning borderline. High-functioning refers to people who can hold a job, maintain relationships, enjoy interests, and engage in the community to a reasonable extent. Low-functioning people tend to find such endeavors overwhelming, meaningless, or even mystifying. Additionally, a person can be generally high-functioning though struggle with specific issues. For example, as an undergraduate I met a teaching assistant from Harvard who had dyslexia and the professor insisted that he read handwritten assignments as a means to contend with his dyslexia. This was a good example of someone who was generally high-functioning, though low-functioning in a specific area that required intense remediation.

This book is written for all borderlines, especially because there is an overlap between high- and low-functioning BPD. That is, the borderline will have good days and bad days—good years and bad years—days when sunshine seems miraculous and others when fresh air feels heinous. Sometimes it is the extremes of highs and lows that creates the greatest sense of powerlessness or hopelessness, robbing the borderline of his ability to enjoy a sense of predictability or certainty in his life.

Whether the borderline is high-functioning or low-functioning, the functioning always occurs in a particular context of behavior, emotion, and thinking. In this book, behavior, emotion, and thinking are inseparable because they influence one another as one interactive system. Thus, trying to understand impulsive behavior without understanding the immediate thought that precedes the behavior is unhelpful. Similarly, investigating a person's feelings without considering interpersonal interaction is incomplete.

Poor Predictability

I never make predictions, especially about the future.
– Yogi Berra

Predicting the general course of BPD is extremely difficult if not impossible, though Freud suggested that past is prologue. In fact, our ability to predict children's progress into adolescence and even adulthood by examining behavior, emotion, and thinking, and even academic ability is modest at best. I was once told by a headhunter that CEOs were generally C students who showed only modest promise, yet they become invaluable because they have multiple skills that they integrate, including dogged persistence. My father almost failed his first two years of medical school, partly because of his inability to memorize huge amounts of information (and he couldn't pull himself away from NHL finals). Nonetheless, he excelled in his clinical work as a fourth-year student and just three years after finishing his postgraduate work he was offered an opportunity to lead an inpatient psychiatric unit. Thus, predicting the life trajectory of even a university student is quite difficult. *Because predictability is so poor, gaining insight about the BPD and life-skills is crucial because in medicine cures are unusual and even more so in psychiatry (although this may change with gene therapy). In healthcare, life expectancy has been extended and quality of life improved not because of direct cures for particular diseases but primarily because of proactive preventative care, including the colonoscopy, nutritional improvements, infectious disease control, antihypertensive medications, gynecology checkups, and related prophylactic care. In the absence of a cure improving behavior, emotion, and thinking through professional therapies—but also education and life-skill development—is crucial for the borderline to lead a dignified and meaningful life.*

Nomenclature

If you do not know the names of things, the knowledge of them is lost too.
> – Carl von Lenne

Rose is a rose is a rose is a rose.
> – Gertrude Stein, *Sacred Emily*

In this book, I generally refer to persons with Borderline Personality Disorder as "the borderline," as syntax oftentimes demands that the word borderline works better than alternative phrasing. For example, the sentence "the borderline may find that he experiences an unstable identity" seems to work better than "the person with BPD may experience an unstable identity" because the former is, I think, softer. (Though perhaps I am wrong. I'm no Hemingway.) I also use the phrase "the borderline" in the majority of cases to personalize the narrative and "borderlines" much less often, though I hope this does not detract from the flow. It's also a sensitive issue because it reflects how the person does or not does not define himself. That is, some borderlines define themselves by the disorder because it can be physically and psychologically overwhelming and energy- and time-consuming. Other borderlines consider the disorder only a small part of their personality or identity because they feel their lives are filled with meaning and wonder separate from the disorder.

The pronoun "he" is used throughout this book—even though most people with BPD are genetically female—and wherever possible the singular will be used. The male pronoun is used to de-stigmatize how this disorder has harmed women and branded them as unstable, erratic, irrational, histrionic, and even psychotic. Moreover, men with BPD are often misdiagnosed as depressed, neurotic, antisocial, misunderstood, or just ignored. The "he" pronoun is used for the above reasons and not due to insensitivity or lack of inclusivity of identity.

My Work

> What we catch and kill we leave behind, but what escapes us we bring with us.
> – Heraclitus

I want to clarify that I'm a forensic psychiatric social worker and non-practicing lawyer (to the embarrassment of my mother) with a background in political science and psychology. I accept referrals because criminal, immigration, or civil litigation lawyers ask me to evaluate cases to more fully explain a client's psychosocial history, including family and mental health issues. Forensics is a ten-cent word meaning court consultant so that persons with special expertise help lawyers and adjudicators where the court wishes to understand various issues, including psychiatric and family matters. Immigration lawyers primarily refer cases so that I can evaluate hardships that American family members will suffer if their non-American family member is forced to leave the United States, though I also evaluate asylum, spousal abuse, competency, and other immigration forensic issues. Criminal lawyers primarily refer cases so that I consider mitigation through a broad psychosocial evaluation to uncover anything and everything to fully explain the criminal defendant's history and how he got into trouble, and to provide a more informed understanding of his judgment and decisions. As such, my practice area is quite different from those who have a traditional clinical psychotherapy practice or psychiatrists who rely on pharmacotherapy as the primary mode of intervention. I'm hoping that this vantage allows for a perspective not usually seen.

A New Look at a Familiar Painting

Ring the bells that still can ring
Forget your perfect offering
There is a crack, a crack in everything
That's how the light gets in.
    – Leonard Cohen, *Anthem*

Many years ago, a friend mentioned that she was visiting an art exhibition by a famous Impressionist painter. She had been to several exhibits of the same artist, and I asked her what she hoped to gain by attending yet another retrospective show. She replied that if she learned even one new thing from one painting in the exhibit that it would be worth her effort. There are many books, podcasts, and online articles on BPD, yet I'm hoping that this book offers helpful information or even wisdom that makes reading this book a worthwhile journey.

The truth is that after decades of research and discussion about psychological injury, psychiatric pathology, and general mental health issues, our ability to explain the etiology or origin of any mental health issue is quite limited. Because many books are available on BPD, which are both extensive and yet not exhaustive, I approach the subject with modesty and humility, as I am aware that much remains elusive. I hope that this book eases the pain of people who suffer from BPD and their families and friends. Any shortcomings in this book are a result of my own limitations.

Finally, everything I write—books on forensics, novels, poems, and even the present volume—is to help me clarify clinical and humanistic ideas that I have thought about for a long time. Certainly, writing this book has allowed me to reflect on what I have learned about BPD, and the opportunity to share my thoughts with others is invaluable for my own growth. (This year I helped my younger daughter study for her biology tests. I told her that she would be ready for the test when she felt confident enough to teach the material to someone else). This book is not meant to be a comprehensive review of BPD, but rather my own subjective understanding based on my limited clinical experience with clients. It is necessarily limited in scope and perhaps even flawed in presentation, though hopefully still valuable to those who suffer with BPD.

PART II

BORDERLINE CRITERIA

I hurt myself today
To see if I still feel
I focus on the pain
The only thing that's real
The needle tears a hole
The old familiar sting
Try to kill it all away
But I remember everything

What have I become
My sweetest friend?
Everyone I know
Goes away in the end
And you could have it all
My empire of dirt
I will let you down
I will make you hurt

I wear this crown of thorns
Upon my liar's chair
Full of broken thoughts
I cannot repair
Beneath the stains of time
The feelings disappear
You are someone else
I am still right here

What have I become
My sweetest friend?
Everyone I know
Goes away in the end
And you could have it all
My empire of dirt
I will let you down
I will make you hurt

If I could start again
A million miles away
I would keep myself
I would find a way.

– Nine Inch Nails, *Hurt*

CHAPTER 2

Conceptualizing Borderline Criteria

Introduction

...and the land was topsy-turvy and darkness covered the deepest of the surface.
— *Genesis* 1:1

It is generally assumed that the various editions of the *Diagnostic and Statistical Manual* (DSM) are based on hardcore research. Research has indeed played a crucial role in developing diagnostic criteria and even new diagnoses, however, politics has also played a role. For example, Intellectual Disability, which was formerly referred to as Mental Retardation, was changed in name because of the stigma. I'm hoping to keep politics out of this book.

I am not going to discuss what I believe are the merits or drawbacks of the criteria of BPD as outlined in the DSM5. There are clinicians who dismiss BPD as a disorder altogether, others dismiss the DSM (present and past editions) as folly, and still others believe that persons diagnosed with BPD have been misdiagnosed so that a serious clinical error has occurred. As far as I'm concerned, what's most important is to focus on the human being whose presentation is often quite nuanced and also to remember that a person can never be explained by research or clinical criteria alone no matter how accurate.

Research without clinically informed empathy is misguided.

Humans are dynamic and changing creatures, so criteria that seem applicable to the person at one point in his life may be completely inapplicable at another point. Indeed, a person may have the ability to abstain from impulsive behaviors all week, attending to daily matters in a responsible way, and yet reserve the weekends for sexual and spending impulsivity with little overt risk to the weekdays that follow. It is also very possible for two people to have BPD and yet their symptoms may be quite different, so they experience the disorder in dissimilar ways. *It's necessary to evaluate and reevaluate not just particular symptoms, but also to consider when they appear, what they mean, and how the person functions in a particular context.* The best way to understand a human being is through a clinical psychosocial evaluation.

The Psychosocial Evaluation

No particle of scattered truth is ever wasted. The harvest will come in.

    – Lydia Maria Child

Germs don't have motives. The answer comes from a patient's personal life. Not from a blood test.

    – David Shore

The psychosocial evaluation is a key strategic tool used by clinicians to elicit information to learn about people and conceptualize general functioning and mental health issues revealing a host of details about the person's life. There are several foci in the evaluation, including:

- childhood experiences (subjective and objective)

- quality of relationships to family members (family dynamics)

- adult development (development is a life-span phenomenon)

- perception of self and other through experiences and interpersonal functioning (identity and self-esteem as understood through object relations)

- influences (home, environment, religion, culture, and values)

- community interaction (education, employment, socialization, and interests)

- medical and psychiatric issues and pathology (both serious and non-serious)

- stressors – traumas, loss, shame, resentment, fear, anger, jealousy, guilt, and challenges (frustrations and disappointments)

- strengths/vulnerabilities – resilience and ego defenses

- core needs, hopes, dreams, values, and trust – drives and motivations.

Although there are multiple other clinical considerations, ultimately it's the clinical psychosocial evaluation that provides what is most important.

For example, inadequate mothering may cause a young child to secrete more stress (cortisol) hormones into the bloodstream, creating an epigenetic change, that is, stable but potentially reversible alterations in a cell's genetic information that result in changes in gene expression but do not involve changes in the underlying DNA sequence. Conversely, an anxious mother in the third trimester may secrete more cortisol which may lead to a more verbal toddler. However, blood and genetic testing will tell you nothing about the *quality* of mothering in the absence of a psychosocial evaluation.

For example, high levels of testosterone do not make people more aggressive, rather it makes them more sensitive to cues that trigger aggression. However, it is impossible to know what those cues are without a clear understanding of the kinds of interpersonal relationships, fears, and anxieties the person harbors.

For example, it is true that oxycodone, which is made in the hypothalamus and controls trust and empathy, can make us more social toward those people who are more like "us" and less social toward those who are not like us (them), but it is only possible to understand "us" and "them" through a psychosocial evaluation.

For example, a child's brain circuitry, including neurons (grey matter) and synapses (connections between neurons), greatly increase in the cerebral cortex and are then gradually pruned throughout adolescence. The insulating myelin on nerve fibers that carry signals between nerve cells continue to accumulate gradually improving neural communication and the adolescent's brain is dopamine-rich. Yet, these changes yield little or no clinical information about the adolescent's daily decision-making and coping mechanisms without a psychosocial evaluation.

For example, the insula cortex may cause us to react with moral judgment, but that can only be understood in the context of a particular person's childhood environment, culture, or religious values, which is understood through a psychosocial evaluation.

The hypothalamus links the nervous and endocrine systems via the pituitary gland and may help coordinate autonomic nervous system functioning controlling hunger, body temperature, and other homeostatic systems, but these systems exist in a particular environment where the person has particular environmental experiences—and this can only be known through a psychosocial evaluation.

Although the psychosocial evaluation remains the gold standard, there are alternatives. In particular, psychologists utilize a variety of psychological tests—most of which are self-report instruments—which ask clients to provide information about their health and well-being. It should be noted that the majority of psychiatric diagnoses are rendered in the absence of testing.

The study of genetics, neuroimaging, and neurophysiology all have merit and can be highly informative, but we humanize the individual and understand his decisions, behavior, emotion, thinking, environment, culture, and family experiences through a detailed clinical psychosocial evaluation. *Absolutely no medical or psychological test can replace the simple question: How do you feel?*

There is one major limitation to the psychosocial evaluation: the clinician can only elicit information that the client is aware of. For example, I was once at a holiday party and saw a single mom leave early with her boyfriend, leaving her young daughter alone and frightened. The daughter became quite panicky and needed considerable support from her older sibling. It's possible that when evaluating the daughter when she is an adult that she will have no memory of this event and thus she may not provide a reliable history about the quality of maternal care that she received. Often, the quality of the psychosocial evaluation can be much improved through a parallel history, that is, by eliciting information from the client's family members. *Because memory is selective and unreliable, it will always prohibit the person from providing a truly complete psychosocial history. As a result, while psychosocial evaluations aim for exactness they often settle for approximation.*

Secret to Clinical Expertise

To describe my life precisely would take longer than to live it.
  – Edouard Leve

In displaying the psychology of your characters, minute particulars are essential.
  – Anton Chekhov

There is a secret to all good clinical understanding: assign clinically significant meaning to seemingly unimportant behavior, emotion, and thinking. That is, the clinician's job is to observe and listen to the person very carefully without judgment and understand that a person's behavior, emotion, and thinking is not just a superficial presentation, but rather communicate or reflect idiosyncratic meaning that provides clinical insight into the person's psychosocial well-being and even psychopathology. (Emotions or feelings aren't necessarily caused by overt thoughts but are constantly foisted upon us by our subconscious based on former experience and how we perceive our environment. We then rationalize the choices that emerge from those emotions and feelings, often turning them into self-fulfilling prophecies. *As such, we use emotional reasoning as evidence that something is true*).

Here's a personal example. I was walking with my daughter and struck my finger. Over the next several days the finger became extremely sore with what seemed like puss inside. Weirdly, there was a dark spot in the middle of the injury. I was concerned that when I struck my finger I got something in it, such as a very small piece of wood, which caused an infection and inflammation. I saw several healthcare professionals, including a dermatologist, explaining what occurred. The problem was repeatedly misdiagnosed. It turned out that it was a wart, which is a small, fleshy bump on the skin (or mucous membrane) caused by the human papilloma virus.

Many skin warts contain one or more black dots near the center, which are in fact visible blood vessels that supply the wart with nutrients and oxygen. A good clinician would have noted the black dot in the middle of the injury and assigned clinical meaning to it. Clearly, it had to be something, and understanding what that something was would provide the key to a relatively simple diagnosis repeatedly missed because the healthcare professionals ignored what was dead center in the injured finger.

Here's another example. In my second internship in day-hospital psychiatry, there was a patient who attended group therapy who would act with subtle moments of impulsivity, such as touching the ID badges of staff members. This was done without animus, aggression, or any other accompanying issue. My supervisor noted that this person could have BPD. I was completely oblivious to this and skeptical about the supervisor's diagnostic ability given such little information. It turned out that the supervisor was correct. It was a crucial lesson about understanding people based on subtle behaviors, but also how a clinician can extrapolate from a seemingly benign action to consider the possibility of more serious problems.

This is not to suggest that every behavior, emotion, and thought belies a symptom of psychopathology, but rather that behavior, emotion, and thinking have a particular meaning to a particular individual given his particular psychosocial history. For example, fidgeting can have multiple meanings depending on who does the fidgeting and even when, where, and how it occurs. For one person fidgeting may signify he has a secret that he wants to share, but he is reluctant to speak about it because of shame; for another person fidgeting may reflect acute anxiety because it is the first time he has ever spoken with a therapist; for another person fidgeting may indicate that he is lying about something; for another fidgeting may indicate a neurological symptom. Moreover, sometimes the reason for behaviors, like fidgeting, may remain unknown even after an extensive psychosocial evaluation.

For this reason, the best clinicians are both clinically as-tute—in trying to understand the meaning behind a person's behavior, emotion, and thinking—and also humble appreciative of our limits in understanding the human condition.

DSM5 Definition and Patterns

If you want a happy ending, that depends, of course, on where you stop your story.
> – Orson Welles

Humans are pattern-recognition machines.
> – William Gibson

The limits of my language are the limits of my world.
> – Wittgenstein

According to the DSM5, a Personality Disorder is an enduring pattern of inner experience and behavior that deviates from the norm of the person's culture. The pattern is seen in two or more of the following areas: cognition, affect, interpersonal functioning, or impulse control. The enduring pattern is inflexible and pervasive across a broad range of personal and social situations. It typically leads to significant distress or impairment in social, work, or other areas of functioning. The pattern is stable and of long duration, and its onset can be traced back to early adulthood or adolescence. The personality disorder subtypes are Paranoid, Schizoid, Schizotypal, Antisocial, Borderline, Histrionic, Narcissistic, Avoidant, Dependent, and Obsessive-Compulsive. This is a verbatim definition of personality disorder. And yet, if the definition is so clear and encompassing, why are clinicians so easily misled into misdiagnosis and how are people with BPD unable to recognize that they clearly have a psychological or mental health problem?

While symptoms are important, the key word is *pattern*.

Pattern is an important concept because it is crucial to recognize specific behavior, emotion, and thinking that exists or repeats over a long period of time so that pathology is indeed recognized in the context of a person's overall functioning. Obviously, pathology can also occur in an acute form. For example, someone can experience reactive psychological trauma or even psychosis after experiencing a sexual assault. At other times, however, pathology is *not* recognized and so patterns are not recognizable even over long periods of time. For example, a person can have a serious medical issue, but because symptoms do not manifest in an overt way, or perhaps because the person's functioning has not altered, symptoms may remain hidden making diagnosis impossible. The consideration of patterns may also help guard against the danger of overdiagnosis and misdiagnosis, which can lead to debilitating stigma and bias. *When the reason or causation for a disorder or disease is absent, patterns of functioning must be considered carefully as a means to understand and help the person.*

BPD is a Disorder

The worst part about having a mental illness is that people expect you to behave like you don't.
  – *Joker* (2019)

BPD is a disorder, or disease, and therefore a serious matter like any medical illness. (Disease and disorder are more or less synonyms. However, disability specifically means that the person is not able to function in a normal manner). BPD undoubtedly has a genetic component. However, there are so many genes at play that there are no specific biological markers, as far as I know. In general, there may be dozens of genes that contribute in different ways to disease processes. I use the word "disease" purposefully, as anyone with BPD will tell you it is truly an affliction. Disease means pathology and disorder is a close synonym. My computer tells me that disease is defined as a disorder of structure or function of the human, animal, or plant, especially one that produces specific signs or symptoms or that affects a specific location and is not simply a direct result of physical injury. This definition fits BPD quite well, especially as there are recognizable patterns of behavior, emotion, and thought that characterize the person at the individual level and also as a category of disease. Still, *the goal is to humanize the person, not label or pathologize.*

Medical pathology is based on empirically physical observable problems with cells and tissues, even at the genetic level. Mental health is different. Nothing can be placed under a microscope or scanned or examined to diagnose a mental health problem except for a postmortem brain tissue examination that may reveal Alzheimer's Disease. Some people conceptualize BPD as having subtypes in which the person's presentation satisfies the general definition of the disorder, but with specific prominent issues, such as impulsivity. BPD can also be conceptualized on a spectrum of criteria and seriousness much as autism has been re-conceptualized as Autism Spectrum Disorder. While this may detract from specificity of clinical description, it also allows for a broader range of symptoms in the areas of behavior, emotion, and thought.

BPD is also a syndrome because it is understood empirically by various criteria and symptoms, which taken together provide a consistent and general recognizable clinical presentation. Although I'm a firm believer that understanding how a person generally functions is just as important as understanding specific pathology (and indeed they are inextricably related), there are moments when exact information is required. For example, when someone overdoses and seeks emergency room help, the healthcare worker needs to know exactly what drug caused the overdose to know what if any treatment should be administered.

Borderlines are sometimes dismissed without sympathy, as they are seen as vying for attention through erratic behavior and unstable moods. However, if the person who presented in this way suffered a catastrophic back injury as a child from an automobile accident, the person would gain sympathy for the rest of his life. Similarly, I have seen many children with ADHD, and often parents or even professionals will say things like "Why can't you just focus?" or "Why can't you just sit up straight and do your homework like everyone else?" However, when the child has difficulty with focus, homework assignments, and socialization because of congenital deafness, the child receives endless sympathy. *BPD is a disorder, or a disease, and persons who suffer from BPD must be afforded sympathy and understanding due to their challenges, deficits, and even disabilities, some of which may be lifelong.*

Complex Trauma Model

People assume you aren't sick unless they see the sickness on your skin like scars forming a map of all the ways you're hurting.
- Emm Roy

Andrew: It hurts.
Allison: Ya.
Andrew: What did they [your parents] do to you?
Allison: They ignore me.
- The Breakfast Club, 1985

If a man's character is to be abused, say what you will, there's nobody like a relative to do the business.
- William Makepeace Thackery

While it's true that BPD can be rooted in a genetic predisposition, other borderlines may experience complex trauma as children. Complex trauma concerns severe and pervasive multiple harmful events—including abuse and neglect (which may even include an invalidating or dismissive environment)—that a child suffers often by immediate caregivers and which causes developmental, cognitive, and behavioral dysfunction, prohibiting self-regulation and leaving the child feeling incompetent, worthless, stupid, inadequate, terrified, guilt-ridden, and insecure with self-blame and shame. This shapes the child's values, including proclivities and judgment, leaving him with an overreactive nervous system, impairment in various skills, often a feeling of physical and emotional exhaustion, and an inability to modulate anger due to a chronic sense of betrayal and distrust. *Complex trauma overwhelms and remains with the person serving as a new psychological foundation undermining safety and trust so that the person feels unbearable sensations related to insecurity, forcing the person to continue to react as if still in danger mobilized to fight or run unable to see others' point of view or coordinate thinking and feeling, even causing devastating physical health issues.*

However, there are several caveats about how people experience trauma. First, the severity of a single harmful incident can be systemically damaging. Second, microaggressions can add up to systemically damaging harm. And third, people perceive and are affected by harm in idiosyncratic ways. For example, my grandparents were in a serious automobile accident and, while both walked away physically unharmed, my grandfather never drove again and my grandmother continued driving until age 80. This is because my grandfather was a child of Eastern Europe anti-Semitism, causing him to become risk-averse, while my grandmother, who grew up in poverty in Connecticut, nevertheless enjoyed a safe environment with wonderful opportunities so that she was in many ways outgoing and a risk-taker.

Developmental Disorder Model

> I can't focus, I'm overwhelmed, I fail courses, I have no friends,
> and I call my parents every five minutes because I feel insecure.
> When I visit home I sleep in my parents bed. I'm a child who
> goes to college.
> – Anonymous

> As power decreases, pageantry increases.
> – Anna Della Subin, *Accidental Gods*

In some ways, the low-functioning borderline (noted above) is similar to someone with a developmental disability who must devote years to learning behavior, emotion, and thinking skills if he wishes to thrive. *BPD is generally akin to a developmental disorder because many of the issues that the borderline contends with match childhood developmental problems, including separation anxiety, attachment issues, separation-individuation, difficulty learning from mistakes, impaired social development, and various related behavioral and cognitive issues—and even oppositional defiance.* This model suggests that the borderline has not adequately achieved milestones associated with appropriate childhood and adolescent development. Clearly, if the child or adolescent has not mastered age-appropriate development, then adulthood almost by definition will be very challenging.

A client once described BPD as PTSD without the T. That is, he felt himself experiencing various symptoms of clinical trauma from childhood (which can have similarities to BPD), though the client recognized that he could not identify specific or general trauma in childhood. He believed that somehow his development was just not on the correct track or somehow derailed and that this in itself caused him to suffer BPD. This is akin to developmental psychopathology, which asserts that mental illness should be understood in part or in whole as development gone wrong.

Autoimmune Disease Model

Body: Something is wrong.

Me: Oh no. Not again. I swear everything is fine.

Body: Something is seriously wrong. I'm going to kill it with fire.

Me: Please don't.

Body as it attacks itself: I'm killing it! Aren't you proud of me?

– Jenny Jones

Another way to conceptualize BPD is as an autoimmune disease, as the body and brain constantly strive for stability and security, even sometimes inadvertently causing self-injury to achieve this goal. In autoimmune diseases, the body's natural defenses attack what it perceives as a foreign invader or unfamiliar substance that should not be there. More accurately, the body cannot adequately differentiate between normal cells—which the body produces for healthy functioning—and foreign cells, which have invaded because of infection or another reason. Autoimmune diseases have probably always existed, although it appears that the numbers have increased in recent decades. (I suspect that various industrial chemicals confuse and poison the body, contributing to autoimmune diseases).

The problem is that the body does not react to unknown cells and substances, but often *overreacts* as the body's immune system is unable to properly identify the foreign invader or substance. When the invader is well-known, such as a common bacteria, the body knows exactly what to do and the matter can resolve in a few weeks or even a few days. But when the body is unfamiliar with the foreign invader a clear strategy is unavailable, leading to sometimes ineffectual or even counterproductive overreactive defensive measures. *Stress, particularly abnormal or overwhelming stress, can cause the body and brain to react or overreact similar to an autoimmune physiological response. It does not matter if the stress is real or perceived as long as the person understands the stress as threatening, frightening, or sufficiently anxiety-provoking.* Sometimes the best defense is doing absolutely nothing at all, allowing the body and mind to properly heal, but with BPD the body and mind overreact and never really stop reacting unless the brain is halted and checked.

Traumatic Brain Injury Model

Make eye contact with me. I am in here. Come find me. Encourage me.

– Jill Bolte Taylor

Traumatic brain injury (TBI)—brain dysfunction caused by an outside source—may result from various harms, though the most common are strokes and violent blows to the head resulting from a sports injury or automobile accident. There may be both immediate and delayed symptoms, some of which can be quite serious, resulting in physical, psychological, social, and neurological limitations or even permanent deficits in the person's life. TBI rehabilitation often requires a systematic approach to allow for proper healing, including psychiatric and psychological supports, occupational and physical therapy, various neurological care, case management, and recreational and vocational supports. Similarly, *whether the origin of BPD is genetic or environmental, it is helpful to conceptualize it as a brain injury, as borderlines benefit from a systemic evaluation of functional limitations and deficits, appreciating that only by tackling problems with an array of supports can substantial improvement occur, allowing for a better quality of life.*

Maybe You're Not So Fucked Up

Beings who are so uniquely constituted must necessarily express themselves in other ways than ordinary men. It is impossible that with souls so differently modified, they should not carry over into the expression of their feelings and ideas the stamp of those modifications.

> – Jean-Jacques Rousseau, *Dialogues*

Today you are you, that is truer than true, and there is no one who is youer than you.

> – Dr. Seuss

Don't assume you have BPD just because you believe you fit the criteria. You may not be as fucked up as you think you are. This is particularly true for adolescents whose raging adrenal, sex, and growth hormones can wreak havoc with behavior, emotion, and thinking that can mimic BPD for several years while the brain develops. (Testosterone, for example, increases ten times in adolescent boys). *There are enough people in your life who want to put you down that you don't have to denigrate yourself, over-diagnose, or erroneously misdiagnose yourself.* There's a *South Park* episode, "Bloody Mary," where Stan's father, Randy, is pulled over by a cop and ticketed for drinking under the influence. Randy then joins an AA group convinced he's an alcoholic, partly because of his hypochondriasis and narcissism. Stan then has to convince his father that he is not an alcoholic, but rather someone who screwed up just once. *Do not self-diagnose and do not overidentify with the criteria of BPD to your detriment.*

Summary

If someone put my feet to the fire, forcing me to describe BPD in a single phrase, I would probably say developmental attachment-behavioral genetic interpersonally-induced emotional-cognitive abnormality, which to my mind is nondescript and clinically unhelpful. For this reason, describing specific criteria of BPD without jargon is crucial and the focus of the next two chapters.

CHAPTER 3

Borderline
DSM5 Criteria

Introduction

This chapter will investigate DSM5 criteria for BPD.

Frantic Efforts to Avoid Real or Imagined Abandonment

> For many borderlines, 'out of sight out of mind' is an excruciatingly real truism. Panic sets in when the borderline is separated from a loved one because the separation feels permanent.
> – Jerold J. Kreisman, *I Hate You Don't Leave Me*

> Obsessed by a fairytale, we spend our lives searching for a magic door and a lost kingdom of peace.
> – Eugene O'Neill

> But that's what fantasies are for. They let you skip the degradation and head straight to the top.
> – David Sedaris, *Giant Dreams, Midget Abilities*

PART I: FRANTIC EFFORTS AND FANTASY

"Frantic efforts" means that the borderline will do things—such as exhibit dramatic or attention-seeking behavior often accompanied by emotional somersaults—to offset his fear of abandonment (and not being loved). Yet, this almost always convinces the other person that the relationship is not worth saving because of the overwhelming energy and time that the borderline demands. The old saying "if you love something set it free" for borderlines would go something like "love for me is rare because who the hell would want me and so I have to do everything possible to ensure that he stays with me because if he leaves I'll crumble into a million little pieces and I won't find anyone else."

The word "frantic" is apt because it emphasizes that the fear is not just psychologically anticipatory, but physical with an obvious bodily response. And, indeed, the borderline may experience a panic attack with various physical manifestations, some of which can linger for minutes or even hours. While the other person may not be fully aware of the borderline's psychological fear of separation, he would probably notice the frantic, physical, panic-like response that the fear of separation induces in the borderline. Thus, *the borderline's panic-like frantic behavior serves as messenger, communicating his anticipatory fear-based reality and fear of separation to the other person.*

The borderline's abandonment fear is anticipatory and often frantic in nature, meaning that, like many anxieties, it is the *anticipation* itself of the abandonment which is the most psychologically damaging and frightening to the borderline. Indeed, when true, permanent separation occurs, the borderline is no longer frantic or fixated on the other person and may accept the reality of the loss, seeking a new caretaker or partner to host his anxiety. Yet, the permanent separation must be truly concrete and final, as anything less causes the borderline to harbor the fantasy that the separation is temporary or that changing his behavior can win back his partner.

This suggests that with borderlines, the quality and nature of relationships needs to be clarified and that once clarified the borderline will not harbor fear of abandonment or not being loved. However, clarification—even very careful and detailed clarification—may not necessarily calm the borderline's anxiety. This is because the borderline's anxiety is based on fantasy or irrational thinking, and the irrationality of the anxiety makes reassurance extremely difficult to achieve.

Fantasy is an important psychological concept derived primarily from psychodynamics. Fantasy is closely associated with children who invent stories about fantastic things, events, and people or creatures as a way to understand the world around them. Borderlines use fantasy as a way to contend with issues in their lives, including anxiety-provoking issues and situations. The problem with fantasy is that it can be so out of touch with reality that people living in the real world find that the borderline's fantasies are simply too wild or bizarre—and self-centered—to encompass. Healthy adults harbor fantasies about power, wealth, love, and much else, but unhealthy adults harbor fantasies as an everyday coping mechanism against overwhelming fear and anxiety. Clearly, if the borderline retains wild fantasies about being abandoned while his partner is tethered to reality, then it's inevitable that the borderline's perception of the relationship will be different from that of the partner's.

The most enigmatic element of all this is that the frantic efforts to avoid abandonment may be most serious not with long-term stable relationships, but rather with transient, less important relationships. One can understand a child feeling separation anxiety from a parent or immediate caregiver, but it would be very unusual (and bizarre) for a child to have separation anxiety from an uncle who he sees only occasionally at family events. Similarly, frantic efforts of losing a boyfriend because of BPD seems to make clinical sense, but why would the borderline have similar frantic fears of abandonment in transient relationships? The answer seems to be that *the borderline cannot adequately distinguish between relationships which are healthy, meaningful, and long-lasting and those relationships that are unhealthy, unimportant, and short-term because of abandonment issues.*

PART II: ABANDONMENT

Frantic efforts to avoid real or imagined abandonment suggest that BPD can be partly conceptualized as an attachment disorder with strong similarities to Separation Anxiety Disorder (SAD). In SAD, the first criterion is recurrent and excessive distress when separation from home or major attachment figures occurs *or is anticipated*. This is very similar to the first criterion of BPD. The second symptom of SAD—persistent and excessive worry about losing or about possible harm befalling major attachment figures—is also often seen in borderlines who harbor constant anxiety that close friends or family who provide them (nonjudgmental) support will vanish from their lives. The next symptom of SAD, persistent and excessive worry that an untoward event will lead to separation from a major attachment figure, is also similar to fantasies that borderlines harbor about losing a close attachment figure. Additionally, the next two symptoms of SAD reflect a child's unhealthy need to be physically close to a supportive caretaker even when going to sleep. These also reflect aspects of BPD. Children with SAD often present with repeated physical complaints and borderlines also tend to present with somatic issues, that is, physical complaints that cannot be explained through medical examination, including gastrointestinal issues, headaches, fatigue, and general aches and pains. Lastly, *some children with SAD have difficulty with object permanence—the understanding that objects and people still exist even when you can't see them—and the borderline may similarly become frantic if he does not have immediate proof that his caretaker or partner has not abandoned him.*

While a healthy child learns that short periods of separation are not damaging and longer periods of separation can be quite enjoyable without the constant supervision from a caregiver, the borderline finds any amount of separation intolerably stressful and seems unable to understand that separation is healthy and can even strengthen the foundation of a relationship. *The difference between SAD and BPD is that the borderline's fear is not developmentally inappropriate, but rather irrational and the borderline's fear is not that the other person (or caretaker) will suffer some untoward incident, but that the borderline himself will suffer being helpless and unable to care for himself alone.* (In contrast, the fear of separation is rational when the borderline acts in a way that consistently pushes the other person away.)

The borderline may resort to behaviors and tactics that seem childlike to prohibit someone from leaving him, which often reflects a deep and pathological need to be physically cared for and emotionally loved. There is nothing wrong with the need to be loved or cared for, but with borderlines the fear is that once abandoned he will be emotionally distraught and physically unable to cope to the point that he may prefer self-harm or even death to being alone. The borderline may also interpret seemingly benign behaviors as indications of abandonment, which of course reinforces the borderline's underlying fear and further causes the other person to doubt the integrity of the relationship. *Imagined fears of abandonment for the borderline not only destroy the integrity of his relationship with his partner, but also undermine the borderline's ability to enjoy the relationship when it is strong and healthy.*

The borderline may be viewed as shallow not wanting to be alone when in fact the distress-intolerance of being alone is a profound fear that affects the very psychological structure of the borderline's sense of self. *For the borderline, abandonment or being alone inherently suggest that he has misbehaved or has committed a wrongdoing, causing him to feel a profound sense of guilt and even self-hatred.* The frantic efforts to avoid abandonment—attachment pathology—help explain why borderlines often have unstable and intense interpersonal relationships with extremes alternating between love and hate.

A Pattern of Unstable and Intense Interpersonal Relationships Alternating Between Extremes of Idealization and Devaluation

I didn't know who would leave or stay, so I pushed them all away.
– Anonymous

The borderline may idealize a boyfriend at one moment and because the borderline feels a momentary pang of insecurity, he will almost immediately demonize his partner as not only inadequate but as the source of all of his woes. So the borderline, who dreads rejection, may sabotage the relationship (not just romantic relationships) and also harbor wild fantasies that cause the borderline to think and behave in a certain way that places the other person in an impossible situation. *For the borderline, rejection can be devastating, but perceived rejection is often worse because it means that he has conjured in his mind myriad scenarios in which rejection is possible.* This necessarily means that the borderline will experience many unstable, intense relationships without healthy (intimate) socialization alternating between extremes of idealization and devaluation. Moving from one unstable relationship to another is physically and emotionally unsatisfying and exhausting, and yet it may provide stability of a dysfunctional ilk to the borderline.

All relationships have an element of ambivalence and judgment (or even threat), yet borderlines cannot tolerate ambivalence or judgment in a relationship because it causes uncertainty and distrust, making the borderline doubt the strength of the relationship. This often prompts the borderline to drive relationships into increasing intensity and instability. *The borderline evokes strong feelings in the other person, causing the other person to feel uncomfortable or threatened and then the borderline, in turn, picks up on that and his emotional instability goes into overdrive.* So why not just dump an unstable boyfriend or end an intense relationship? Because the borderline is often quite intense and emotionally unstable and so he feels more comfortable interacting with others that match his internal psychological chaos. Indeed, borderlines sometimes thrive in relationships where there are extremes of behavior, emotion, and thinking. When a tuning fork vibrates at a specific frequency, it shatters glass. That isn't good for the glass but the tuning fork cannot vibrate at any other frequency unless a physical change is made to the tuning fork (or the glass is removed from the tuning fork's reach). *Thus, the borderline's instability and intensity are made more tolerable by interacting with others who confirm the chaos or instability of his own internal world.*

In the borderline's all-good-all-bad world, there has to be a villain, and if a bad guy isn't available for the part, then a bad guy needs to be created. This serves a special psychological need and sometimes the person who provides the most psychological support is the safest scapegoat (particularly if the borderline has a small social circle). At some point, the borderline will get his wish and his partner will become the bad guy. This can take a heavy psychological toll on the partner who is unable to tolerate the borderline's erratic behaviors and unstable moods. *The partner can be anyone, even a parent, yet at some point the partner will become emotionally and physically exhausted, and this tends to occur at the point when the partner feels that his personal dignity has been diminished to the point that he is no longer a partner, but an unappreciated and undervalued caretaker.* The partner may pull away or even experience a stage of grief as he comes to terms with the reality that he can never be a valued member in the relationship. When the borderline's idealization of the relationship crumbles chaos ensues, as the borderline turns to profound cynicism and disenchantment feeling hate towards his partner and distrustful of his own judgment.

My favorite professor as an undergraduate student taught American politics and provided enthralling lectures on Tocqueville and the *Federalist Papers*. Many years later I wanted to read his books so that I could still feel connected to him. I was saddened when I discovered that he had written very little. Just because he was a great lecturer didn't mean that he was a great writer and, although disappointed, it wasn't a big deal because I had warm memories of his lectures. But a borderline may become extremely distraught or even feel betrayed that the professor did not produce any lasting written works and react by sending emails devaluing the professor while also sadly devaluing his own positive memories. *The borderline does not seem to have the capacity to enjoy the very best part of a relationship and the very best memories retained from it. Rather, he idealizes or devalues the relationship to such an extent that even the positive parts of the relationship are insufficient fulfillment for him.* The need to idealize or devalue others in unstable relationships is substantially rooted in the fact that the borderline suffers from chronic identity disturbance.

Identity Disturbance

It will be faithful realism, at least. Stammering is the native eloquence of us fog people.
- Eugene O'Neill, *Long Day's Journal Into Night*

Each me is the enemy of all the others.
- Pascal, *Pensées*

Our identities are a composite of personal appearance, friendships, family, culture, endeavors, productivities, education, and employment. Identity (including sexual identity) is also formed by stress both benign (social contagion) and toxic (peer pressure). If you know what you want to do every day and who you wish to interact with, then identity—or self-concept—should be self-evident.

With identity disturbance the borderline peers into the mirror and it's like looking through fog as he does not get clear feedback, and so the borderline strives to understand his identity in various ways, often by experimenting with relationships and behaviors, some of which may be quite self-destructive. (Some borderlines also experience body dysmorphic disorder in which he has a preoccupation with one or more perceived defects in his physical identity or appearance that are not observable or appear slight to others.) A common misconception is that borderlines hate life, as supposedly reflected in their impulsive-destructive lifestyle. This is not true and many borderlines love life more than other people because they are aware of just how fragile life really is. Often the borderline suffers from identity disturbance because he is disappointed in himself and may even harbor self-loathing but loves life and even desires to participate in various activities, hoping for a feeling of accomplishment and enjoyment. However, when a person's identity is unclear, and he then hates himself, it's impossible for him to participate in activities with any sense of enjoyment because the person that he's with—himself—is constantly there.

Because the borderline lacks an empirical sense of self, he is always trying to achieve a sense of self that is never truly possible, which is an extremely frustrating and anxiety-provoking endeavor. There is nothing more frightening than not having an identity, as it makes some people feel soulless, resulting in existential angst and a bleak way of seeing life. Moreover, borderlines tend to have a fragile sense of identity (or ego) to begin with, and fragile things can be shattered quite easily. And once shattered, regaining coherence and identity stability can be daunting if not impossible.

The borderline may have a very poor understanding of his identity and yet must contend with his personal issues each and every day. It's like going against an enemy you can readily recognize in some ways, but in other ways you just don't know him at all. As such, the borderline may be quite accomplished by objective standards, but by subjective standards he deems himself a failure.

Often, the borderline has never felt comfortable either in his own skin or in a particular home or environment. The borderline may find the task of achieving a healthy and stable identity all the more challenging because he may feel that his identity as a child was not grounded in positive experiences or by supportive caretakers and so there was nothing positive on which to build. *There is only one thing worse than not knowing who you are, and that is knowing you are the result of solely negative experiences and memories.*

The essayist Montaigne asked *que sais-je*: what do I know? Montaigne wanted to bring everything back to its most basic, empirical starting point in an effort to distinguish between what we truly know and what we assume. Without any firm answers from earlier in his life and without any firm answers looking directly into a mirror, the borderline's identity remains painfully elusive and so the borderline strives to achieve an idealized self, which must be constructed—but constructed from what and how? *Whatever self-knowledge the borderline has is elusive, providing few constructive details of his identity and leaving the borderline without an empirical starting point.* Thus, the borderline's chronic experience of anxiety due to identity disturbance leads him to search for answers in impulsively self-destructive and self-defeating ways.

Self-Damaging Impulsivity

> No, no, the adventure's first, explanations take such a dreadful time.
> — Lewis Carrol, *Alice's Adventures in Wonderland*

> Why is it that one runs to one's ruin? Why has destruction such a fascination?
> — Oscar Wilde

Impulsivity—a cousin of disinhibition—is rapid, unplanned or poorly planned decisions without concern for the immediate or long-term consequences of the behavior which may cause potential or real harm, including irresponsible spending, unhealthy sexual encounters, substance abuse, reckless driving, and binge eating, among others. *Impulsivity is not so much about an uncontrolled appetite but rather a knee-jerk reaction.* However, it is wrong to think that the borderline's impulsivity is behavior-driven alone, as it is almost certainly also cognitive in origin—that is, the borderline's impulsivity is driven by impulsive racing (or even incoherent) thoughts that can only be satisfied through the impulsive behavior. While the behavior may or may not satisfy a particular feeling or need, it is often part of an ongoing pattern of behavior.

While we generally want children to be endlessly curious—even impulsive—to discover the world, experimenting with behavior, emotion, and thinking, borderlines (as adults) must learn to show restraint in these areas. While kids are time-blind (and sometimes obligation-blind), adults have commitments, deadlines, and time-sensitive duties. I would distinguish the impulsivity that borderlines exhibit from impulsivity noted in persons with Attention Deficit Hyperactivity Disorder (ADHD) in various ways. While borderline impulsivity is related to emotional dysregulation, ADHD impulsivity is a neurological dysfunction and behaviorally driven without being qualified by anxiety or emotional dysregulation as such. It also seems that the impulsivity in ADHD is generally less dangerous or risky, although this is not always true. Additionally, there is a strong tendency for most children to grow out of impulsive behaviors while adults with BPD tend to exhibit impulsive behaviors in a somewhat consistent pattern throughout adulthood.

Impulsivity may lead the borderline to live on the edge, engaging in dangerous behavior, sometimes even to the exclusion of healthy endeavors. In fact, impulsive behavior can take on a life of its own and become a discreet issue, or pathology, with far-reaching negative consequences for the borderline. For example, at some point frequent impulsive gambling becomes indistinguishable from a gambling compulsion, just as chronic insomnia due to depression may need to be understood as a sleep disorder. Although rock climbing has a high incidence of mortality, it is wrong to assume that most rock climbers are borderlines or that rock climbers are impulsive by nature. To the contrary, endeavors such as rock climbing often require considerable preparation and each move must be considered in a careful manner to remain safe.

Although impulsive behavior may be high-risk and dangerous, it nonetheless tends to allow the borderline to enjoy solace in a way that normal, healthy endeavors usually do not, as it tends to reduce his sense of emptiness, boredom, and even psychological pain. It is not clear if the solace is produced through the behavior itself or by the end result. That is, does an impulsive sexual act satisfy the borderline because of the sexual encounter (the nitty gritty of the interaction) or because of the satisfaction gained from the outcome (the orgasm or similar result)?

This leads to a puzzling question. *If the borderline engages in healthy and safe activities (such as hobbies) that bring enjoyment, solace, and a personal sense of accomplishment, then why would the borderline also need to engage in impulsive high-risk activities which jeopardize his safety and which may ultimately negate his ability to engage in the enjoyable, healthy, and safe activities?* Part of the answer lies in the recurrent, destructive, and even suicidal nature of the borderline's personality.

Recurrent Suicidal Behavior, Gestures, Threats, or Self-Mutilating Behavior

> Being suicidal isn't about wanting to die. It's about quieting the pain inside, losing the epic fight against a mind that begs you to die. Suicide isn't because of being weak. It's because someone tried to be strong for too long.
>
> – Anonymous

Suicidal behavior and gestures or threats or self-mutilating behavior may or may not be related to one another. Suicide is really a sub-topic under the general rubric of self-harm or self-injury. The large majority of people who engage in self-harm have no intention to end their lives or even to try to end their lives. Harmful behavior can be wide-ranging, including chronic drug abuse, high-speed driving, dangerous or high-risk hobbies, or self-destructive tendencies. Of those people who contemplate suicide, relatively few will ever attempt or even follow through although the single greatest indicator of a completed suicide is someone who has previously attempted suicide. It is not uncommon for people who consider existential questions to also consider the merits of suicide and yet very few seriously consider ending their lives. Thus, it is important to differentiate between fantasy, or existential considerations, and true suicidal ideation, which is associated with real clinical issues—although the two may overlap.

Suicide is extremely complicated because people kill themselves for different reasons under different circumstances with different mental health issues—and even with different tools—and geography, culture, and gender also play important roles. There are certainly people who kill themselves accidentally, such as an accidental overdose, and others who behave in such a consistently self-destructive or dangerous manner that the likelihood of dying is substantially higher than normal, or perhaps even inevitable, as with rock climbers who do not use gear to secure their safety.

Suicidality may be either active or passive. Active suicidality occurs when a person has a plan to end his own life, such as by a clear overdose of medications or even street drugs. Active suicidality is characterized most often by deep psychological pain or despair and a hopeless belief that nothing in the person's life can improve in a meaningful way. Passive suicidality concerns thoughts of death or dying that may include the person stating that he wonders what it would be like never having to wake up (sleep and sleep and sleep) so that his pain would vanish. Thus, passive suicidality is usually more ideational while active suicidality is often accompanied by a thought-out plan or impulsive behavior that may or may not be realistic or even coherent.

As such, some people calculate what behavior will eliminate pain short-term and long-term. This may sound odd to someone who has not experienced overwhelming psychological or physical pain, but when pain levels are chronically high, all hope seems lost and personal meaning and dignity become extremely difficult to maintain. I believe that the healthcare system (and physicians) has an obligation to minimize pain and when pain is chronic and overwhelming—and multiple interventions have been utilized without success to alleviate the pain—the person should be allowed to end his life rather than contend with endless suffering. While suicide is generally rooted in hopeless feelings of despair with deep psychological pain often associated with clinical depression, borderlines are first and foremost disappointed in themselves and the belief that their own behavior, emotion, and thinking is awful and repetitive.

Self-cutting, which is not uncommon among borderlines, is sometimes viewed in the same category as recurrent suicidal behavior, but the reality is that it probably exists as a separate phenomenon (even though self-cutting can lead to death if the cuts are deep and the wounds are placed in water to prevent blood clotting). Borderlines often make gestures, threats, or engage in self-harm behavior for years without ever being admitted to inpatient hospitalization because the behaviors are not immediately life-threatening or even seem benign, particularly when it involves superficial cutting on the forearm or thigh.

Self-harm can have both an objective and subjective component. For some people tattoos are a form of mutilation but for many tattoos are a form of art that allows for positive self-expression and even beautification. For some people drugs serve as a gateway to mind enhancement and for others drugs serve objectively as a form of physical self-harm. (Clearly, anyone who associates the word "recreational" with drugs does not consider drugs especially harmful). My wife bought me a pain mat that has plastic needles and sometimes I fall asleep on it waking up with redness and even puncture marks. Lying on the pain mat distributes pain in the body more evenly, it may block specific pain areas, and it is thought that the pressure from the needles stimulates the muscles releasing endorphins and tension, allowing for better circulation and even neurological functioning. While I subjectively find my wife's gift relaxing, some people would view the result as unnecessary bodily harm, especially if over-the-counter sleep aides or calming music are equally effective to induce sleep.

For borderlines, threats of self-harm and self-mutilating gestures regulate emotions, alleviate feelings of emptiness, or provide relief against self-hatred. It may allow for personal control, it may serve as a way to punish oneself for perceived wrongdoing, or it may serve to gain attention or to simply "feel something." Many borderlines would just as soon be dead unless someone can affirm their need to remain alive, so deep is their need for human recognition of their psychological and emotional issues. What's most clear is that this category pertains directly to affective instability due to marked reactivity of mood.

Affective Instability Due to a Marked Reactivity of Mood (E.G., Intense Episodic Dysphoria, Irritability, or Anxiety Usually Lasting a Few Hours and Only Rarely More Than a Few Days)

PART I: AFFECTIVE INSTABILITY

Calm waters run deep.
– Latin Proverb

The joys of love made her human and the agonies of love destroyed her.
– *Star Trek*, S3:E19

Affective instability refers to uncontrolled, rapid, and intense changes in mood sometimes noted by a maudlin display and usually due to an anxiety-provoking external issue. As adults we want to believe that we have the capacity and freedom to choose our destinies through decisions that we construct as individuals based on our needs, desires, hopes, and wishes. If we don't feel we're in control then we cannot know who we are and we cannot influence or alter our pathway. The borderline often feels out of control—that is, he literally feels that he is not able to direct his life in a meaningful way but rather perceives somehow that other people or circumstances control him in a manner that leaves him feeling helpless and even worthless. *Living with the perception—which creates feelings that causes behaviors—that the borderline cannot control his life or even his needs is devastating and maddening, and can cause affective instability.* This prohibits the borderline from enjoying a sense of security in his life, which is essential to enjoying certainty and predictability, which in turn, of course, allows a person to feel safe and stable to begin with. Without a sense of control, it is no wonder then that the borderline experiences unstable moods.

Affective instability—along with impulsivity—means that the borderline may not be responsible for negative outcomes. A person who crashes his car during a seizure, which is basically an electrical storm in the brain, is not held responsible because he is not in control of the neurological synapse misfiring that caused the seizure to occur. While a person with a seizure disorder may not be ethically responsible, he may be devastated to learn that the neural misfiring robs him of self-control and perhaps even personal dignity and safety. *The inability to control mood can be just as debilitating as the inability to control behavior or thinking.*

Borderlines exhibit affective instability for many reasons, including significant reactivity of mood. Reactivity is a crucial word because it's clear that in many instances the borderline is reacting to an external stimuli that the borderline perceives as overwhelming or threatening, causing him to alter his mood. The borderline's reaction tends to be out of proportion to whatever caused the feeling of unease and onlookers are often baffled and feel quite uncomfortable at the borderline's reaction. It is not clear why some borderlines change moods and not change something else. For example, when most people feel threatened they do not change their mood, but rather their level of anxiety or even physically remove themselves from the danger or cower in some manner. Moreover, the border-line's mood may shift on a dime without apparent rhyme or reason, which makes the borderline feel that he simply does not understand his own emotions. It doesn't help that the borderline often thinks in black-and-white terms without the ability to properly perceive nuance so that the mood instability is accompanied by extreme thinking. Perhaps the most serious issue with BPD is the cumulative effect of various symptoms which find expression at the same time and inform one anoth-er almost always in a negative fashion, and often accompanied by intense anxiety.

PART II: INTENSE ANXIETY

Being broken doesn't mean that you don't have a cohesive nar-rative.

– Ocean Vuong

Mood and anxiety are related but separate phenomena. One of the challenges of a clinical evaluation is to understand person-al and psychiatric issues as clearly as possible. Most persons with psychiatric issues are dual-diagnosed and the large ma-jority of borderlines suffer from depression and/or anxiety. How someone could live with BPD and not have intermittent episodes of clinical depression or anxiety is unfathomable.

Borderlines may experience acute anxiety due to various fears, including abandonment, social awkwardness, and patho-logical doubt—but also the inability to tolerate even moderate levels of stress that occur due to mundane change. If the border-line experiences a pattern of acute anxiety, then the borderline may also experience intermittent panic attacks. Panic attacks occur when there are discreet periods of intense anxiety pre-cipitated by either a frightening thought or anxiety-provoking issue and which are recurring and unexpected (although not always). Panic attacks are characterized by a sudden frightening sense of being out of control with a wide variety of physical symptoms including heart pounding, sweating, trembling, sensations of shortness of breath, chest discomfort, nausea or abdominal distress, hot or cold sensation, numbness, lightheadedness or dizziness, feelings of unreality, and fear of loss of control or even death. Many people with panic attacks also suffer with other somatic issues, that is, physical complaints that do not have a specific medical explanation, such as recurrent headaches, general aches and pains, loss of hair, reactive dermatological issues such as rashes, and various gastrointestinal issues. Finally, the borderline's anxiety may also manifest through obsessional thoughts (endless rumination) or even compulsive behaviors. When the obsessions and compulsions complement one another repeatedly it can be quite similar to Obsessional Compulsive Disorder (OCD). Thus, BPD is often accompanied by clinical anxiety that can manifest in various ways. The borderline's reactivity of mood and anxiety due to uncertainty and general sensitivity to perceived threats is also closely associated with his sense of emptiness.

Chronic Feelings of Emptiness

When you're empty inside you will end up in some crazy places, but you will still be lost.
  – *White Lotus*, S2:E6

You can sit in an enormous restaurant where you don't know anybody and where nobody knows you, and you don't feel all the same that you're a stranger. And here you know everybody and everybody knows you, and you're a stranger. A lonely stranger.
  – Anton Chekhov, *The Three Sisters*

Chronic feelings of emptiness (for some, longing may be a better word) are an especially challenging aspect of BPD because the borderline is often unable to articulate what emptiness means, the quality of emptiness, or even how it manifests. It can be so elusive that it may be glossed over by clinicians. Feelings of emptiness are probably related to identity disturbance, that is, the borderline is out of touch with or unaware of his identity (or nature or needs), harbors a poor sense of self-concept, is plagued by self-doubt, often feels ripped off or taken advantage of by others, and even worthless and helpless so that he feels horribly unconnected and untethered, lost like a rudderless boat. The borderline may have enjoyable and safe interests, such as sports or the arts, and yet fulfillment from these endeavors is not sufficient to quell chronic feelings of emptiness. In fact, it is not unusual for a borderline to enjoy pride and even fulfillment in his external accomplishments and yet maintain an inner sense of emptiness.

Chronic feelings of emptiness tend to cause the borderline to feel that he always needs more of something and is never satiated, filling the void with attention, sex, drugs, or food, though filling the void can be a lifelong endeavor in futility. Sitting at home with a delicious meal reading an engrossing book with everything you need may seem to most people like an ideal moment to cherish, but the borderline's chronic feelings of emptiness preclude true enjoyment even when everything seems to be going exactly right.

For some borderlines feeling empty may equate to a sense of profound inner loneliness or perceived social isolation. It is odd that even when surrounded by friends and family, the borderline's sense of loneliness may not diminish. In fact, feeling lonely when surrounded by friends and family may reinforce for the borderline the profound constant emptiness that he endures.

To feel nothing, that is, to experience inner emptiness is awful and to feel something—anything—is often much preferred. For some borderlines, emptiness feels like being born without a soul and it may be preferable to have something or *anything* to replace the empty vessel. True emptiness can cause feelings of horrible desperation because of the empty vacuum and it is tempting to take a chance even on those things that are negative or outright destructive in nature.

Paradoxically, the borderline's profound sense of emptiness may evince a sense of entitlement as a means to proactively stave off feelings of powerlessness or perceptions that he is being taken advantage of by others. As a result, others may view the borderline as narcissistic or even manipulative, especially given the borderline's demand for recognition and even admiration.

The borderline may experience chronic feelings of emptiness as dissatisfaction and disappointment with his personal choices or inability to find meaning in his endeavors. The borderline's emptiness may be related to a particular kind of existential meaninglessness or anxiety with his own life experiences. *Borderlines may philosophize about existence and the pain of being alive, believing that everything is ephemeral and without certainty or permanence. This sense of futility and emptiness can be maddening and perhaps related to bouts of uncontrolled anger.*

Inappropriate, Intense Anger or Difficulty Controlling Anger (E.G., Frequent Displays of Temper, Constant Anger, Recurrent Physical Fights)

Hurt people hurt people.
– Anonymous

The borderline's emotional volatility and intense anxiety may be accompanied by intense anger—or even caustic rage—especially when he feels acutely frustrated or perceives being degraded or even just misunderstood. Intense anger or rage can be energy consuming and emotionally overwhelming accompanied by yelling and even displays of physical violence.

Indeed, during moments of intense rage, the borderline may be so out of control that he may require physical restraint to ensure his own safety (or the safety of others). When the borderline feels that he has no internal sense of control (emptiness) and also exhibits no outward sense of control (impulsivity), life can be hellish, and it can rob him of his personal dignity. *Controlling mood and anger can help the borderline avoid burning bridges with friends and family—and survive his own tyranny.*

Borderline inappropriate and intense anger is akin to temper tantrums in truculent children. When children display temper tantrums, it's often in response to acute feelings of frustration. Temper tantrums, and even moments of rage, are considered developmentally appropriate for young children (and even adolescents), though rarely appropriate for adults unless specifically provoked. Parents who have seen their children throw temper tantrums (and every parent has) never quite get used to it, but understand that it occurs in the context of a child's acute frustration, and so the parent weathers the storm. However, when an adult becomes enraged, friends and family can become quite frightened and even disgusted by the display, even though the moment of rage may be seemingly unavoidable and uncontrollable to the borderline.

Most aspects of BPD exist in an internal framework that can be quelled or even hidden from the outside viewer, but when inappropriate and intense anger occurs the borderline is often overwhelmed to the point that all of his defenses melt away and his deepest negative thoughts and feelings emerge in a manner that can be quite unsettling even to someone familiar with that person or BPD. Intense anger and intense behaviors may not exist together, so that the borderline may experience intense anger (quietly seethe) and yet show no outward behaviors that suggest inner turmoil, but if you scratch just underneath the surface (that is, if the borderline is provoked) you discover profound and intense rage, so that when it is externalized it explodes like a bomb.

The borderline who has displayed bouts of intense anger since childhood may grow up to find that his immediate family still contends with his issues as they did when he was a child. They may be reluctant to confront the borderline or challenge his outbursts because it is a constant in the family's life. Family members know that borderline rage is like a tornado and sometimes it's best to take cover, allowing the storm to pass without provoking the borderline to further anger. Family members may also have been traumatized by past outbursts so that when the adult borderline becomes enraged, it triggers horrible memories from earlier years.

The borderline who experiences intense anger, anxiety, personal and interpersonal disappointment and frustration, emptiness, and confusion may feel that he is at war with himself and even the entire world so that he is out of touch with reality, as indicated by transient stress-related paranoid thoughts.

Transient, Stress-Related Paranoid Ideation or Severe Dissociative Symptoms

When everyone is out to get you, paranoia is just the next logical step.

> – Dr. Johnny Fever, *WKRP in Cincinnati*

Reality is important, but it's not for everyone.

> – Anonymous

PART I: PARANOID IDEATION

Paranoid thoughts are types of delusions. A delusion is defined as a false belief based on an incorrect inference about external reality which is firmly sustained despite what almost everyone else believes and despite what constitutes incontrovertible and obvious proof of evidence to the contrary. The borderline's paranoid ideation may occur where he believes or fears he is victimized or sees others as the enemy, often without rhyme or reason. The delusion may cause the borderline to be suspicious, guarded, grudge-holding, hypersensitive to criticism, preoccupied with loyalty and betrayal in relationships, or fearful that others harbor evil motives, and this leads the borderline to have low trust in others—or even himself—causing severe interpersonal conflict due to an argumentative and defensive or oppositional stance.

While some delusional thoughts are due to acute stress, others are ingrained into the borderline's thinking so that he operates within a delusional system. Delusional systems are maintained by a set of roughly logical connected delusions whose inner reason keeps them secure. Over long periods of time, false beliefs and delusional systems may even provide solace and predictability. Stress-related paranoid ideation is less serious because it usually occurs within a specific context due to an external stimuli and after a short time the delusional thinking abates. However, with systemic delusions, the borderline's everyday decision-making and interpersonal relationships are informed by the delusional system, which can be quite destructive in nature. The borderline may truly feel that he is losing his mind, and the reality is that his thoughts are in fact generally out of touch with reality, which makes dealing with the real world an incredible challenge.

While the borderline may suffer transient delusions, he may also experience more serious forms of psychosis. "Psychotic" means out of touch with reality and it is often typified by hallucinations (false sensations) and delusions (false beliefs). Hallucinations are generally well-identified because there are only five kinds based on the five senses—visual (sight), auditory (hearing), gustatory (taste), tactile (touch), and olfactory (smell). In contrast to hallucinations, delusions can be extremely varied and idiosyncratic with dozens of different kinds of false beliefs that may manifest in nuanced ways. Some paranoid ideation—such as the belief that there is a camera in the television—is relatively more concrete than a person who has a generalized delusion that people may be following him. Delusions often involve magical thinking (the idea that one's thoughts and words can influence others or even the world in some meaningful manner), ideas of reference (where the person believes that irrelevant things in the world pertain to him), or delusions of identity (where the person believes that his identity has been fractured, stolen, or misplaced in some manner), which is more common in borderlines because of their unstable, insecure, or fragile sense of self.

With delusional thinking, subjective perception—although misplaced or even wrong—is in some respects more important than objective reality. This is because, although we live in a real (objective) world, our subjective perceptions tell us who we are and how to interact with others in our environment. Obviously, if we are using a kettle to sweep the floor, we want to be told that the kettle is for boiling water and the broom is for sweeping. However, *the borderline's subjective understanding of himself and others is just as important as objective reality because the borderline primarily understands the world through his own perceptions. While the borderline is often blind to his own unconscious hostility he is often paranoid and hypersensitive to the hostility of others, often provoking reactions, including dissociative symptoms.*

PART II: SEVERE DISSOCIATIVE SYMPTOMS

I begin with truth and end in myth. When prose falls apart poetry ensues. The poem is the debris.

    - Ocean Vuong

Borderlines with dissociation experience a cognitive breakdown—or lack of cognitive continuity—that involves disruptions in thoughts, memory, awareness of surroundings, identity, or perception. It would seem that some people (voluntarily) use dissociation as a defense mechanism to stave off anxiety. Flight and fight responses are believed to be an atavistic response to immediate danger when our ancestors lived on the Savannah Plains in Africa. I've hiked a few times and unexpectedly seen bears, and yet I never considered running away because it would be useless and I never considered fighting the bear because it's obvious that I would be killed. However, dissociative phenomena have two related issues that are real and important: fawning and freezing. Fawning essentially means engaging with the threat, placating it so that it becomes less threatening by matching the expectations or desires of the threat. Freezing means momentarily shutting down, perhaps even holding your breath, hoping that the threat no longer sees you as a threat. *While fawning is about tactical engagement, freezing is about tactical disengagement.* It is also crucial to note that rage itself can be dissociative. That is, rage (as opposed to anger) can result in the loss of cognitive orientation because it can be so overwhelming.

Conclusion

This chapter focused on the DSM5 criteria of BPD, however, there are a wide range of other criteria not included in the DSM which is explored in the next chapter.

CHAPTER 4

Non-DSM5 BPD Criteria

Introduction

At one time it was believed that life could only survive within a defined spectrum. We now know that life can exist in extremely hot (even boiling) and below-zero temperatures. Life can exist with or without oxygen and with or without light. Life exists in volcanoes, at the bottom of the pitch-dark ocean, and space vehicles have returned to Earth with bacteria withstanding extremely high temperatures upon reentry. Almost everything exists on a spectrum and this is especially true for healthcare issues. BPD exists as a general category with people experiencing most if not all of the symptoms at one point or another, but more often than not people experience the symptoms with a wide range of severity and, for several months, a person may experience only a few of the symptoms in a milder form or not at all.

This chapter will identify major issues in BPD that are omitted from the DSM5 criteria. The criteria in this chapter are both the outgrowth or consequences of criteria noted in the previous chapter, but also distinct criteria in their own right that require serious consideration. *A symptom should reflect any behavior, cognitive, or emotional issue that helps better identify a larger pattern within a syndrome or disorder, leading to a clearer and more accurate diagnostic picture.* It is hoped that the symptoms or criteria noted below add greater clarity and exactness to BPD.

Cognitive Dysregulation

Cognitive symptoms in BPD have not received sufficient research attention and they are not accounted for in current neurobiological theories.
– Joel Paris

I may be damaged, but I'm not confused.
– Anonymous

Cognitive dysregulation generally concerns difficulty processing information, learning or retaining new information, confusion, poor focus, and memory loss or dysfunction. Memory is how the brain (unconsciously) encodes (metabolizes), processes, and retains information for future decisions and judgment about behavior, emotion, and thinking. Memory is critical for self-reflection allowing to build an identity through time and experience. In general, human memory is quite fallible and a core characteristic of trauma is that it may imprint a memory that cannot be forgotten. Trauma is something that cannot be unseen or unfelt and posttraumatic stress disorder is a pathology of forgetting. *We generally forget or do not remember the vast majority of information that we perceive and yet we sometimes encounter situations where a memory is unforgettable, often to our detriment.*

For borderlines, cognitive dysregulation may also include impressionistic perception, leading to imprecision or exaggeration or distortion of meaning and difficulty discerning nuance. Borderlines may also have difficulty inferring someone else's thoughts or intentions, leaving them feeling socially awkward. Some borderlines are so preoccupied with certain negativistic or morbid ideas that they essentially become obsessional thoughts that swirl around like an eddy, prohibiting focus on those things that are truly important. In general, humans are error-prone due to assumptions, biases, and prejudices and this is certainly true for borderlines due to cognitive dysregulation. *Ultimately, cognitive dysregulation may limit the borderline's ability to fully and accurately understand himself and others, think through problems, and it may result in poor judgment and rash decisions, leaving the borderline feeling foolish, scatterbrained, ignorant, and socially awkward.*

The most serious consequence of cognitive dysregulation is that it causes disorganization in daily life, prohibiting the borderline from strategic planning, problem-solving, and adaptation, which are key to personal development and success. (Destiny is comprised of careful planning and random chance).

The motto "the harder I work the luckier I get" sounds smart, but hard work requires cognitive skill and organization, and people who suffer from cognitive dysfunction and disorganization cannot make their own luck and therefore cannot assume control of their lives. *If you can't strategize then you can't organize, plan, or problem-solve because you can't juggle ideas even when the issue is immediate and serious—and the inability to strategically plan due to cognitive dysregulation can completely undermine the borderline's life, leading to behavioral dysregulation.*

Behavioral Dysregulation

I suck at life. I'm inelegant.
    – Anonymous

I have always depended on the kindness of strangers
    – Blanche Dubois, A Streetcar Named Desire

Cognitive and behavioral dysregulation complement and reinforce one another, magnifying the negative effects of each. (Poor or limited physical functioning is most often the result of neurocognitive or muscular deterioration due to a genetic disorder, disease, aging, and even various viruses and bacteria). Most people, when they set their mind to something, can undertake short-term tasks with relative ease and, although long-term projects may require greater effort, with proper planning these goals can also be met. Yet, some borderlines don't really get through the day at all and essentially do not function, living their lives without a career, interests, or personal development, unable to attain either short-term or long-term goals, causing chronic feelings of frustration, anxiety, and even profound personal disappointment of being a failure.

Someone who suffered horrific abuses in her childhood once told me, "I just suck at life." This was a woman who could provide insightful input when discussing various psychological issues and yet she could not get her life together in a meaningful way—that is, she could not progress from step to step or accomplish much of anything other than holding a menial labor job. Paradoxically, because of behavioral and cognitive dysregulation, some borderlines actually become obsessive about having a controlled and orderly life, perhaps because the borderline feels that anything less will cause his world to fall apart. One way that borderlines gain control is by limiting or monitoring the kind and amount of food they eat or reject, which may lead to an eating disorder. This is especially serious when the borderline's erratic eating patterns are reinforced due to depression and anxiety, which may also draw attention to the borderline's internal pain. For some, anorexia is not a desire to be thin, but a desire to look ill or to engage in self-punishment. *Behavioral dysregulation or dysfunction clearly has a planning and strategic component, but without self-knowledge and self-love healthy progress can be only incremental at best. When both cognitive and behavioral dysfunction are present, so is psychic pain.*

Psychic Pain

You get distracted by pain. It leaves less room for the things you don't want to think about.
> – *House*, S2:E12

Neurosis is a substitute for legitimate suffering.
> – Carl Jung

Get at the pain.
> – Coco Johnson

You know that pain and guilt can't be taken away with the wave of a magic wand! They're the things we carry with us, the things that make us who we are. If we lose them, we lose ourselves. I don't want my pain taken away. I need my pain!
> – Captain James T. Kirk, *Star Trek V: The Final Frontier*

While pain often accompanies medical disease and physical injury, pain also accompanies psychiatric illness and psychological injury. Borderlines try doggedly to understand why life is so painful, weighing apparent evidence and sometimes inventing explanations—and sometimes even asserting that they feel pain more intensely than other people do. BPD is characterized by emotional and psychological pain so much so that it is impossible to help the borderline without understanding his psychic pain. While emotional pain pertains to hurt feelings (damaged emotions) psychological pain pertains to something more akin to brain pain, that is, neurological pain, which is the pain that we feel when we strain to process information, trying to make sense of the world. At times, emotional and psychological pain can be difficult to differentiate from physical pain—and indeed pain is always neuro-physiologically based even when initiated by an external stimuli. *It is literally painful to feel lonely, misunderstood, abandoned, empty, confused, embarrassed, and not in control of your own decisions, so it's important to never discount a person's perceived level of physical or psychic pain.*

The borderline may recognize his psychic pain by psychological and emotional cues (crying, increased confusion, irritability, distress, and agitation), by observing changes in movement (rigidity, tension, fidgeting, restlessness, increased pacing/rocking), changes in activity patterns (aggressive, resisting care, disruptive, and withdrawn), and verbal and nonverbal complaints (grimacing, moaning, crying out, or cursing). Psychic pain is often the borderline's lifelong companion and it can leave him feeling breathless, as *psychic pain robs the borderline of psychological and emotional energy.* Pain can prohibit proper cognitive processing—and may even lead to total confusion—because it's impossible to think through situations or anticipate danger when pain is overwhelming. Staying healthy requires hard work and may even be a full-time job for those with chronic physical pain, and the same is often true for psychic pain. *Behavior and cognitive dysfunction cause pain and pain can cause behavior and cognitive dysfunction, which feeds into the borderline's poor sense of self-preservation.*

Poor Sense of Self-Preservation

I'm really bad at listening to other people, even to smart people, and even when they have really good advice for me.

    – Anonymous

I Love Life. I Hate Me.

    – Anonymous

Another crucial corollary to cognitive and behavioral dysregulation is that the borderline tends to exhibit a poor sense of self-preservation due to poor decisions. It is not only that the borderline has a tendency toward self-injurious behaviors, but that he just seems to have a limited ability to meaningfully distinguish between what is generally helpful from what is unhelpful and safety from danger. When you approach an intersection without a stop sign or streetlight, you slow down or dart your eyes from side to side to check if cars are approaching. The borderline seems less concerned or aware of such dangers or of life's challenges, not because he necessarily wishes to cause himself harm, but because it's just not on his radar or a priority for reasons that are not fully understood. Rafting down a river's rapids requires basic self-preservation, avoiding dangerous rocks jutting out from the river, though everyone gets a thrill from occasionally bumping into one of the rocks. But the borderline cannot steer clear of the rocks, may even enjoy getting thrown from the raft into the current, and cannot navigate a safe pathway. *Without a good sense of self-preservation, the borderline is always in harm's way, resulting in the need for a pity party.*

Pity Party Due to Perceived Victimization

Self-pity is easily the most destructive of the non-pharmaceutical narcotics. It is addictive, gives momentary pleasure, and separates the victim from reality.
　　– John W. Gardner

When asked why do you always wear black I reply because I am mourning my life.
　　– Anton Chekhov

It's a dog-eat-dog world and I'm wearing Milkbone underwear.
　　– Norm, *Cheers*

Pity party mode—defined as constant complaining of victimization—causes self-centered thinking, reinforces negative bias about growth and healing, increases the risk of depression and anxiety, prohibits personal responsibility, and is anti-motivational. The borderline pities himself, wallows in his sorrow, asserts that he is marginalized, and wants pity from everyone else because of his supposedly desultory life of helplessness. The borderline is reluctant to process emotions because they are threatening causing anxiety, so he chooses to indulge in pity party, which is a false (emotional) state. People don't pity successful people, so the borderline may proactively ensure that he remains in a pitiable situation, at least superficially. Paradoxically, the need for pity may cause the borderline to set himself up to experience disappointment, failure, abandonment, or even abuse. For example, this may occur when the borderline establishes unrealistic expectations in a relationship dooming it to fail, allowing the borderline to make himself a victim and then go into pity party mode. While an ordinary person may write a love letter, the borderline may write a love letter with tiny hearts on every letter, pouring his soul into the note, creating such impossibly high expectations that anything but a full commitment by the recipient will cause the borderline to feel completely letdown and foolish. The borderline may also assert that while he would do anything for anybody nobody would do anything for him.

Parties require preparation and invitations are sent out for guests to respond and show up. Similarly, the borderline's pity party needs a method to put people on notice, that is, various attention-seeking behaviors. The borderline may feign or exaggerate medical or physical symptoms (Munchhausen Syndrome) as a means to gain psychological or emotional support (Factitious Disorder), and may even falsely assert that his child has medical or physical issues (Munchhausen-by-proxy). Both can be effective in gaining medical evaluation but rarely lead to proper psychiatric support.

Many borderlines have either been victims of abuse or perceive themselves to have been victims. In the mind of the borderline, particularly at the unconscious level, the difference between the two may have little practical significance when it comes to the pity party. When the borderline has grown up in a middle-class home with all the attendant luxuries that one can objectively hope for there may be little reason to pity him. In fact, some may view the borderline as terribly narcissistic and unappreciative of his childhood support system. In reality, however, it's impossible to know what really goes on in a home unless it is understood by someone who actually experienced it and lived there. Abuses may be more common in lower socioeconomic neighborhoods, but it's naïve to think that it doesn't exist in middle-class families and neighborhoods.

Someone can be both a victim desiring pity and a victimizer at the same time, perhaps because the person uses cognitive dissonance to compartmentalize his experiences. That is, it's possible for the borderline to be manipulated by others truly deserving pity while also being horribly manipulative toward others.

Manipulation and Coercion

> Manipulation becomes emotional blackmail when it is used repeatedly to coerce us into complying with the blackmailer's demands, at the expense of our own wishes and well-being.
> — Susan Forward

Sometimes the only way for the borderline to understand or control his internal chaos is through the manipulation and coercion of others. Manipulation and coercion may also occur when the borderline feels he is inadequate or fears abandonment and therefore drastic control is required to ensure that the relationship is maintained. Manipulation and coercion, which are basically various forms of control, can include mental cruelty, social and emotional isolation, taunting, degradation, false allegations (often due to jealousy), pressuring (often due to anxiety), relentless criticism or minimizing the other person's abilities (often due to low self-esteem), inducing fear, shame, anxiety, intimidation, threats of self-harm, control of property, and demeaning actions. Sometimes the target of manipulation and coercion becomes a personal servant attending to all of the borderline's physical and instrumental needs often because the borderline has a history of irresponsible behaviors, including alcohol or drugs, and poor overall self-care.

Borderlines who are manipulative and coercive can also be alluring and even seductive given their impulsive and risk-taking lifestyle. Like high-calorie sugar-laden processed foods, the borderline can be quite addictive given the reinforcement of pleasure for the partner. And yet, like maintaining a diet of processed foods, it may ultimately yield negative results physically and psychologically leaving the partner feeling used and unwell.

When the borderline's partner is not in control the borderline may feel less crazy and isolated because he can relate to the other person's dysfunction, though the borderline most often does not intend to hurt his partner or the target of his manipulation or coercion. The manipulation and coercion is often directed at someone that the borderline suspects is susceptible to manipulation and coercion (just as a psychopath targets particular rather than random people). However, it's not that the borderline does not lack empathy but rather the borderline does not always have sufficient capacity to empathize with others given his confused internal world and inability to empathize with his own issues. *As such, the borderline may act in a manipulative or coercive manner, though without animus or evil intent toward others.*

The borderline is not a narcissist (though the borderline must stop the compulsive storytelling of his life because no one cares). In fact, the borderline rarely has a genuine grandiose sense of self-importance but rather feels quite poorly about himself. The borderline is rarely preoccupied with fantasies of unlimited success or ability, as he often feels quite powerless. The borderline does not truly believe that he is special but rather empty and unloved, and the borderline does not require excessive admiration but rather excessive understanding because of his fragile identity. However, the one area where the borderline does appear narcissistic is with regard to interpersonal exploitation, that is, taking advantage of others for personal gain. While the narcissist and psychopath tend to exploit others for personal gain, which may be pecuniary in nature, the borderline tends to be manipulative and coercive to fulfill psychological needs and ensure emotional stability. (It is somewhat akin to the difference between malingering and factitious disorder; malingering is undertaken most often for pecuniary gain while in factitious disorder the person's symptoms are feigned for psychological or emotional gain).

Manipulation and coercion of others is almost always a struggle in the short-term and impossible to maintain long-term, but it may allow the borderline a transient sense of stability and security in a world where he usually experiences instability and insecurity. Nobody likes to be manipulated or coerced because there is an invasive dishonesty from the abuser. Anyone who uses manipulation and coercion as an everyday part of interpersonal interaction clearly either has no understanding about how healthy relationships function or healthy relationships are unimportant to that person. Additionally, such a person most likely does not enjoy a healthy relationship with himself and may even manipulate or coerce himself into situations that are unsafe or unhealthy. Until the borderline has the ability to adopt honest introspection, external (interpersonal) honesty will also remain difficult to achieve.

The most serious problem occurs when manipulation and coercion serve as the borderline's normative method of interpersonal communication and interaction with a key person in his life. This is because the recipient will in time become aware of the manipulation and coercion and pull away from the borderline or provide very negative feedback that will cause the borderline overwhelming anxiety knowing that he is about to be alone again, leaving him hypersensitive to rejection and loss.

Hypersensitivity

What you see and what you hear depends a great deal on where you are standing. It also depends on what sort of a person you are.
— C.S. Lewis, *The Magician's Nephew*

Some borderlines seem to have a protective guard due to their "raw skin" so that when they feel the least bit threatened, judged, or criticized, a protective shield is activated. Hypersensitivity is a symptom but also a defense against threatening triggers.

Borderlines who experienced childhood trauma needed to be paranoid-hypervigilant against danger to protect himself or others, which then became an ingrained mode of acting and thinking in adulthood. I first became aware of this with people who were incarcerated, as they needed to adopt a healthy dose of paranoia to stay alive in prison. I have also seen this with sexual-orientation asylum cases with people who had to exist in a paranoid state to remain physically and psychologically safe in a homophobic society, yet the person never rids himself of paranoid thinking even years after living in the United States. I evaluated a gay refugee from Bangladesh who refused to live in New York City because of what he called "the gay scene." He noted that keeping his guard up in Bangladesh was easy because his guard could never be let down, while he felt that being only sometimes careful in New York City was impossible. As such, the client chose to live in a more conservative community in Upstate New York where he would continue with his hypervigilance unabated.

Borderlines and persons with Autism Spectrum Disorder share certain characteristics and issues. Like borderlines, a person with autism may have a particular sensitivity to noise, touch, sound, taste, and smell and even to people (or animals) in his immediate surroundings partly because of perceptual problems, even though these elements pose no immediate objective threat. Also similar to autism, a borderline may have difficulty communicating his needs or understanding another person's communication or intentions. Under such circumstances, empathy for self and other is very difficult to achieve. Indeed, some borderlines find everyday banter and chitchat baffling or annoying due to hypersensitivity and anxiety. *The borderline, like the person with autism, must learn to decode his sensitivity and how to navigate his environment or risk remaining overwhelmed all of the time.* As a result of hypersensitivity, the borderline may find that contending with overwhelming thoughts and feelings is only possible vicariously by projecting thoughts and feelings unto somebody else.

Projective Identification

Who wants to see life as it is, if they can help it?
– Eugene O'Neill, *Long Day's Journey into Night*

I'm quite certain that mental health experts reading this book (assuming that any of them even crack the cover) will be less than thrilled that I added criteria for BPD not found in the DSM5. They will be particularly irked when they discover that I've added project identification, splitting, and diffuse or weak ego-boundaries as criteria—all of which allow the borderline to partially or fully disavow unwanted thoughts and feelings. Projective identification, a defense mechanism understood in the context of psychodynamic theory, is a rather unusual issue in mental health and quite particular to BPD. As noted above, a symptom should reflect any behavior, cognitive, or emotional issue that helps identify a larger pattern within a syndrome, leading to a clearer and more accurate diagnostic picture.

Projective identification allows the borderline to contend with anxiety-provoking or perhaps even overwhelming thoughts and feelings by vicarious identification through another person, usually someone with whom the borderline has a close connection. Rage, for example, can be an overwhelming feeling and even potentially dangerous. It is more psychologically economical for the borderline to identify with someone who contends with rage (in a healthy or unhealthy way) as a means for the borderline to contend with (and maybe even understand) his own rage. Sometimes the borderline consciously chooses a partner or friend in a relationship where projective identification is possible. At other times, the borderline finds himself in such a relationship without conscious planning and uses the relationship to his advantage to contend vicariously with his own psychological issues. *Because the borderline does not have the mature cognitive or ego-defensive tools to critically consider or contend with his own negative thoughts and feelings, he may become hypercritical and impatient with the person with whom he experiences projective identification, creating a love-hate relationship.*

A middle-class woman in her thirties was stealing prescription pads from her father's office and giving them to her drug-addicted boyfriend who forged the signature and sold them on the street. The woman remained in this destructive relationship with the drug-addicted boyfriend because he had extremely low self-esteem and self-destructive behaviors just as she did. She did not have the emotional capacity to consider her issues and so she vicariously contended with these matters through her boyfriend's psychological dysfunction and personal devaluation.

Splitting

> My wife is always angry so I don't have to be angry. It works out great.
>
> – Anonymous

Psychic pain that is shared is more bearable than pain suffered in silence.

    – Daniel Paul

If I am I, because you are you, and you are you, because I am I, then I am not I, and you are not you. But if I am I because I am I, and you are you because you are you, then I am I and you are you, and we can talk.

    – Menachem Mendel of Kotzk

While projective identification is a defense mechanism and symptom that often occurs in the context of a single interpersonal relationship, splitting can occur in a single relationship (dyad) or multiple relationships, allowing the borderline to maintain contradictory ego-states even given his fragmented sense of self (and other).

There are different ways to understand splitting. *The borderline uses splitting because contending with unconscious conflict is psychologically overwhelming and so the borderline splits aspects of his conflict, such as love and anger, into extremes comprised of idealization and devaluation,* although the process can be quite subtle. One day the borderline may idealize his partner as the greatest person in the world and on another day devalue him with vicious verbal abuse. Yet, one of the cornerstones of healthy maturity is understanding that almost everyone has both negative and positive qualities, thus seeing the world in a gradient of shades without anger, and accepting that in some ways this is the most beautiful part of being human.

Splitting also occurs with multiple individuals. For example, a child with BPD may view one parent as all loving and giving and the other parent as neglectful or even abusive, so that the borderline does not have to contend with the unconscious conflict and reality that all caregivers have both positive and negative qualities. *The borderline may even play off the two parents against each other, ultimately causing both parents to become emotionally exhausted and useless as caretakers.* Projective identification and splitting—ultimately mechanisms of denial to stave off unwanted thoughts and feelings—often mean that the borderline suffers from weak or diffuse ego-boundaries.

Weak Ego-Boundary

Don't invent sufferings you have not experienced, and don't paint pictures you have not seen.
- Anton Chekhov

God damn you, stop shoving your rotten soul in my lap.
- Eugene O'Neill, *The Iceman Cometh*

There is something beautiful, touching, and poetic when one person loves another and the other is indifferent.
- Anton Chekhov

Borderlines have weak or diffuse ego-boundaries, often struggling to understand where their needs, thoughts, feelings, and identity start and stop in relation to other people—not unlike Woody Allen's social chameleon character *Zelig. Weak or diffuse ego-boundaries can lead to a wide range of identity disturbance and interpersonal problems, including enmeshment with someone else.* Projective identification and splitting used by the borderline helps to promote—or at least complement—the diffusion of his ego-boundaries and may even cause the borderline to feel better about himself seeing someone with similar problems who is even worse off, and perhaps even struggling to survive. When weak or diffuse ego-boundaries occur, the borderline may become overly influenced and deferential, allowing the other person to control the borderline to his detriment. In fact, the borderline may interpret even a small glance from someone as meaningful and mistake it for a genuine connection or even a veiled threat

Weak ego-boundaries have many secondary negative issues, as it often leads to feelings of envy and even jealousy. For example, jealousy is a normal feeling but with borderlines the jealousy is not only a feeling but something that connects with the borderline's identity and needs. When we feel jealous because someone has an expensive car, we may enviously wish that we own the car, the money to pay for the car, or even a better job that would give us money to buy the car. However, the borderline's jealousy and envy can be pathological in the sense that it reflects not only his feeling of desire but fundamentally affects how the borderline defines himself, and as he relates to and idealizes others through mimetic desire.

Mimetic desires are not biological or instinctual drives but rather desires framed by the needs of others, who we perceive as having a higher or special status, hoping that the person will guide us to that desired goal. For this reason it can also be difficult for the borderline to choose something he desires on his own because the borderline craves validation, confirming that his desire has value or meaning. This can lead to anger, rage, low self-esteem, self-incrimination, and intense frustration, and the borderline may even feel so intimately connected with the expensive car that he may ingratiate himself into the life of the owner as a means to become part of the car owner's life and identity. (A great example of pathological jealousy is the character Jonathan Corliss in the movie *A Kiss Before Dying*). When the borderline is unable to satisfy or contend with deep feelings of jealousy, he may feel such contempt for the other person—barely able to hide his disgust—that it may be necessary for the borderline to create an artificial identity to fit into the other person's world. *As such, weak or diffuse ego-boundaries may create for the borderline a false sense of attachment and belonging that almost inevitably causes disappointment or even danger.*

Another major problem with weak or diffuse ego-boundaries is that the borderline tends to overshare his thoughts and feelings. The borderline may feel that when he does share thoughts and feelings he is misunderstood or that his thoughts and feelings are improperly used by others against him. *In failing to retain a private identity, the borderline feels that parts of him are chopped off and he will sometimes share inappropriate thoughts causing others to feel uncomfortable or embarrassed.*

Another corollary of weak or diffuse ego-boundaries is that the borderline tends to have strong feelings or opinions on issues that may be quite unrelated to the borderline's life, as he overidentifies with other people's issues. The borderline then inserts himself into someone else's affairs and assumes he can help when in fact he can barely care for himself. For example, borderlines tend to identify with social equality issues, often advocating for justice and fairness because the borderline's own internal world is marked by chaos and perceived internal imbalance or injustice. (Interestingly, Plato's conception of justice focused on the internal cohesion of different parts of the person). *Borderlines tend to have strong opinions, do not suffer fools gladly, and can become easily distracted when his sense of right and wrong is challenged.* Thus, maintaining internal psychological cohesion and contending with weak and diffuse ego-boundaries is sometimes best achieved through privacy without which social awkwardness may emerge.

Social Awkwardness

I'm always apologizing like I've done something wrong even when I've done nothing wrong.

– Anonymous

George: I can sense anyone's pain.
Jerry: Can you sense any pain now?
– *Seinfeld*, S2:E9

Social awkwardness is a close cousin to social anxiety and often presents in similar ways for borderlines. This is not irrational, but rather quite rational as the borderline appreciates that his cognitive and behavioral dysfunction necessarily makes him socially awkward, which is a marked fear or anxiety about one or more social situations in which the individual fears being exposed to scrutiny by others. Some borderlines will avoid chitchat or meeting new people; they may wish to eat or drink unobserved by others, offer a superficial social veneer to try to fit in, and may avoid public speaking and other similar performances in which they fear they're being criticized or judged. This is particularly true if the borderline has a history of being socially bullied perhaps experiencing a negative feedback loop in social situations.

The major difference between the borderline's social awkwardness and social anxiety disorder is that the borderline's social awkwardness may be rooted in the borderline's inability to decipher social cues while social anxiety disorder is generally rooted in fear of social embarrassment. Borderlines often have difficulty picking up on social cues and indeed failing to do so may result in personal embarrassment and even further social rejection. The borderline may have difficulty deciphering social cues for several reasons. Similar to autism, the borderline may have difficulty deciphering receptive verbal language (or what my younger daughter once called "auditory dyslexia") and/or body language. Additionally, the inability to decipher social cues may be based on the borderline feeling so overwhelmed with his own social awkwardness that he cannot adequately focus on the subtleties of anyone else's verbal or body language communication. This may cause the borderline to simply avoid certain people, places, or even activities. *Often, the borderline is quite aware that he is socially awkward—or even inappropriate without an appreciation of interpersonal boundaries—making other people uncomfortable. When this occurs, the borderline may turn inward and remain very quiet.*

Quietness

> When I'm quiet it's because I have nothing to say. I'd rather let the emotions storm inside me than say the wrong thing and hurt you. Asking people if they are mad at me is too hard.
> – Anonymous

> Unpleasant feelings alone do not cause suffering, it's being alone with those unpleasant feelings.
> - Matthew Lederman

There is a misconception that borderlines act in an overtly impulsive and uncontrolled manner with racing emotions and thoughts, and that he is hell on wheels. However, it is clear that borderlines come in all shapes and sizes just like depression or diabetes can manifest in various ways. Perhaps the least recognized type of borderline is the "quiet borderline." *The quiet borderline contends with his problems in a quiet and private way, rather than acting out in the public sphere or demonstrating overt anxiety, fear, and sadness for all the world to pity his struggles.* In fact, there are many borderlines who are too often misdiagnosed with clinical depression (Major Depressive Disorder) or dysthymia (Persistent Depressive Disorder), or perhaps viewed as simply withdrawn or introspective because of the quiet presentation. The most dangerous medical issues are those that people don't tell their doctors about, causing the issue to remain ignored for years without medical attention until it becomes unavoidably serious at which point there may be nothing that can be done. Here are a few examples of what a quiet borderline may say to remain quiet even though his situation may be dire:

I prefer a little me time = I feel desperately alone

I want to disappear = I want to be found

No one wants me = I don't even want myself

I'm fine = I'm not fine, I need help

I'm just tired = I'm exhausted beyond words

I'm exhausted = I want to kill myself

Sometimes I just need time to be alone and think = Give me one reason to live

I already ate = I'm starving myself

Go away = Show me you care enough to stay away

Go away = Show me you care enough to ask me again in five minutes

Go away = Just one more rejection will kill me

I don't know what I would do without music and poetry = I feel nothing

I'll stay out of trouble = Trouble follows me like a shadow

I'll be careful = I wish safety was my priority

I'm just cold = I don't want you to see my scars

I'm better, I promise = I've never been this bad

I'm okay = I just want to die

You don't understand me = I can't even understand myself

I don't understand what you're saying = I'm too over-whelmed with my crazy thoughts and feelings to have the capacity to listen to anyone else

I'm trying to take it slow = Every moment is painful

I can handle it on my own = I want someone to figure it out for me

These are heartbreaking examples of how the quiet borderline will poorly or not fully communicate his needs or, even worse, minimize the terrible pain that he suffers because he does not believe anyone can understand the magnitude of his suffering. After all, it may seem mysterious and inexplicable even to himself, as the symptoms can be inexact, and so he prefers to contend with his issues in an unassuming way. *Sometimes the borderline feels that being left alone or even lying about his issues is no worse than having someone attend to his issues in either an unhelpful or unsympathetic way.* The squeaky wheel gets the grease and the quiet borderline is often greaseless and must contend with his issues in a private and painful way. The quiet borderline is often alone in his thoughts and terribly bored.

Boredom

Routine, repetition, tedium, monotony, disorder, boredom, angst, ennui—these are the true hero's enemies.
– David Foster Wallace, *The Pale King*

Idle hands are the devil's playthings.
– Proverb

I feel as if I have been in the world a thousand years, and I trail my life behind me like an endless scarf.
– Anton Chekhov, *The Seagull*

Boredom, which may manifest as procrastination, is somewhat related to inner feelings of emptiness noted in the DSM5 but boredom is also separate and requires consideration in its own right. While emptiness generally refers to the borderline's inability to properly understand his personal needs or feel anything of meaning, *boredom involves feelings of apathy or ennui in both the immediate and existential sense and may be accompanied by a flat affect, dreary mood, and even task avoid-ance.* It's not simply that the borderline experiences boredom, but the borderline often feels that other people are boring or uninteresting and when that occurs the borderline may seek to eliminate boredom through euphoric activities. The opposite of boredom is euphoria, which is also a hallmark symptom of bipolar disorder in which the person experiences expansive moods and behaviors marked by inflated self-esteem or grandiosity, decreased need for sleep, talkativeness or pressured speech, distractibility, and involvement in goal-directed or impulsive activities some of which may be purposeless.

Boredom and emptiness sound like benign symptoms, but they are often the most serious. Indeed, boredom may be the brain's signal that something just isn't right. This is because continued boredom, especially when combined with feelings of emptiness, leads to chronic restlessness and unease, which may lead the borderline to impulsive, dangerous behaviors due to a lack of fulfillment and pleasure in his everyday life.

Anhedonia

I used to feel sad and now I'm just numb.
　– Anonymous

Many borderlines suffer from anhedonia—the inability to derive enjoyment from normal daily activities—which is a key component of Major Depressive Disorder. Impulsive behaviors such as sex or drugs allow the borderline to experience pleasure, filling a deep hole of emptiness and boredom with external sources of superficial support. However, these impulsive behaviors do not provide real or lasting meaningful enjoyment to the borderline and the borderline may indeed feel even more empty, alone, bored, and numb having engaged in impulsive pleasure-seeking behaviors, reinforcing for him that these activities have no lasting value or purpose. *Anhedonia is included as a symptom because often the borderline seems unable to enjoy his daily life in a meaningful and healthy way in the absence of empty or dangerous activities, sometimes due to a lack of insight.*

Lack of Insight / Alexithymia

Plans are useless, but planning is indispensable.
– President Eisenhower

Generally, borderlines have poor insight, little self-awareness, and can identify their problems in only a superficial or concrete way. The reason for this is unclear, though generally people with psychiatric issues find it very challenging to provide clear answers as to why they have mental health problems. The lack of insight and even confusion make it very difficult for borderlines to accept long-term psychiatric, family, and social supports. *Without a modicum of insight, healthy decisions and planning are almost impossible.*

A related problem for borderlines is alexithymia, which is the inability or difficulty to identify or describe one's emotions—often coupled with concrete thinking—and especially bodily sensations connected to emotions. This limits the person's introspection even when his behavior, emotion, and thinking seem somewhat clear to others. For example, the borderline may experience acute anger though he cannot verbalize why the anger is occurring at that moment and he cannot explain what triggered the anger from the moment before. This causes the person overt frustration and sometimes results in externalized emotional outbursts. Alexithymia may also limit the person from properly identifying behavior, emotion, and thinking in others, making a proper empathic response difficult and sometimes causing social awkwardness and interpersonal misunderstanding or friction. *The combined lack of insight and inability to verbalize or describe emotions often prohibits borderlines from accepting help even from professionals and this can lead to catastrophic thinking.*

Catastrophic Thinking

> I don't think I catastrophize because I'm negative. I think I catastrophize because I don't think.
> – Anonymous

Although related to cognitive dysregulation, catastrophic thinking is noted here because it is a core issue with BPD and deserves its own consideration. Catastrophic thinking involves ruminating about worst-case outcomes even when there is not sufficient evidence to suggest that catastrophe is at hand, and this can create a self-fulfilling prophecy of doom. It can be a paralyzing issue both in moments of relative calm and certainly in a crisis situation. In catastrophic thinking, the borderline essentially convinces himself of the worst possible outcome by using reason, utilizing every possible negative issue and outcome while neglecting to consider every possible positive issue and outcome. The borderline's thinking can be very narrow, parochial, and non-inclusive. *Catastrophic thinking is often time-specific, occurring in the here and now because when fears are considered with flexible thinking over many hours or days the worst-case scenario may indeed be one conclusion, but thoughtful consideration will lead to the possibility of many others as well, including positive outcomes and even survival strategies, making the worst-case scenario untenable.* Catastrophic thinking and similar cognitive dysfunction often provoke responses from others so that the borderline can gain a sense of security and validation.

Provocation and Validation

> I pick little fights to test people.
>   – Anonymous

Borderlines often purposefully provoke responses through attention-seeking behavior but also due to unintentional cognitive and behavioral dysfunction that causes other people to respond with bewilderment, anger, caution, frustration, and other reactions. *While the borderline is weary of negative reactions from others, fearing that he will fall apart, the provoked feedback also confirms his existence, allowing for a sense of security and validation about his needs and identity, even sometimes confirming that he is alive.*

Conclusion

Both the DSM5 criteria and those identified in this chapter make it necessary for the borderline to establish clear life strategies to maintain his health and safety, which is the focus of the next chapter.

PART III

CHAPTER 5

Surviving BPD

Dignified Survival and Maybe Happiness

The human mind is programmed for survival, not truth.
  – George Santayana

The best revenge is living well.
  – *Seinfeld*, S2:E7

My brain? That's my second favorite organ.
  – Woody Allen, *Bananas*

Like an electrical circuit, the events that occur in the nervous system are morally neutral and only adopt meaning when the resulting behavior, emotion, or thought occurs in the context of particular cultural mores. We are cultural and political creatures and our brains, which can change and even adapt responding to various stimuli, considers immediate and past experiences to predict and estimate the immediate future to ensure safety and stability. The brain is sensitive to the narrative the environment is telling it. The brain essentially regulates and coordinates systems in the body in response to various sensory information sent from different parts of the body and the immediate environment. From this, the brain provides a narrative of sensory experience based on the body's functioning. This story—our emotions—strives for homeostasis but also considers if there is something wrong internally or within the environment. However, our brains are not built to produce happiness, as happiness is an artificial construct. There are certain external cues that may cause a person to experience amusement or contentment, but happiness must be created and re-created each and every day. There are complex systems to protect us (as best as possible given pervasive dangers in the environment and our own stupidity), but no physiological system produces happiness. The brain likes reason (as opposed to logic), but it is not reason that is always useful or protective in our everyday lives. Survival and happiness require considerable effort, and the borderline certainly has his work cut out for him. As a result, happiness must be pursued as a value in and of itself—and it is achieved through endless curiosity and humility, cultivating positive life-affirming choices.

When someone is angry at himself or disappointed in his own behavior he is really angry at his brain, which encompasses the person's personality and identity but it also encompasses far more. The brain makes billions of automatic and unconscious biological decisions, only a small fraction of which we are aware of and which we have any control over. Even professionals with high degrees of technical skill and know-how (such as engineers, physicians, and social workers) are unaware of the vast majority of the brain's decisions. As such, hacking the brain is far more effective than chronic self-hatred because self-hatred does nothing to tackle the underlying neurological functioning that dictates how we behave, feel, and think. You are not your brain and your brain's tyranny can be tamed and even domesticated into a harmonious duality with your identity, ultimately making self-anger and disappointment superfluous—and self-control a reality.

As a borderline, if you really care about social pressures, external validation, and what others think about you, you won't stand a chance to be either stable or happy. Certainly, a person may live a safe and stable life and still never experience happiness or perhaps even contentment. *Yet, for some borderlines achieving stability and safety is a major win and it may yield a good quality of life even if happiness remains elusive.*

Additionally, *the borderline can have both a bad brain and agency. That is, the borderline may indeed suffer from a disorder that affects behavior, emotion, and thinking but that does not preclude the borderline from enjoying stability and even happiness by taking ownership and control of his decisions and the trajectory of his life by identifying positive supports and perceived dangers.* One of the best ways to do this is by identifying triggers.

Identify Triggers

There is anger in the word danger.
> – Anonymous

Best way to avoid punch... No be there.
> – Miyagi, *The Karate Kid*

Triggers—external stimuli in the form of perceived threats such as fear of rejection or abandonment—for the borderline may lead to overwhelming anxiety or even explosive rage. The borderline is highly sensitive to others and his surroundings, causing him to feel uncomfortable or threatened and quite often socially awkward. Anticipating anxiety-producing situations is often routine for most people. I avoid roller coasters because of a few bad experiences. I may be missing out on a lot of fun, but I have chosen to sacrifice the possibility of thrill rides for a feeling of safety, keeping my feet firmly planted on the ground (and my food in my stomach). This means that the borderline must develop a good understanding of his likes and dislikes, fears and anxieties, and supports versus non-supports.

You cannot identify triggers or change what you don't understand, though when you do understand something you become empowered. Consider problems from every side, allowing for nuance, openness, and even vagueness. Always avoid assumptions. Consider how you associate one thing with another while also considering the possibility that these associations are tangential and even unreasonable or illogical. Understanding valid and helpful associations and connectedness between ideas, including interpersonal contexts, can be extremely helpful, but it requires a huge amount of patience, emotional energy, and effort. Similarly, seemingly unimportant behaviors or benign compulsions exist for a specific reason, and trying to make connections to figure out why a particular behavior emerges can add invaluable insight, no less than understanding why a particular feeling is important.

The law provides behavioral structure to almost everything in society, making lawyers who understand and apply the law powerful and needed. Similarly, understanding your own personal psychological rules will allow you to master yourself. For some borderlines it can be helpful to self-impose rules of behavior, emotion, and thinking to assist with better functioning. We all do this in simple ways, such as forcing ourselves to go to sleep at an appropriate hour, but for borderlines this requires rules that also take into consideration maladaptive and destructive behaviors. Identifying dangers—real or perceived—is important because it serves to proactively avoid situations that cause the borderline to spiral out of control. However, *the downside to anticipatory proactive behaviors is that the borderline's list of perceived dangers may grow to such an extent that he becomes overly cautious, isolated, lonely, and even phobic. The borderline must learn to understand that he constructs reality in a very personal way and only then can he understand the meaning that he attributes to behavior, emotion, and thinking—and only then can he attain stability and happiness.*

Avoiding and anticipating problems is a key area that helps minimize errors in hospitals and doing so has clearly cut down on negative incidents that cause patient injury and even serious harm. A helpful idea lies in identifying the most important or relative seriousness of dangers. Quality assurance experts in hospitals made an amazing discovery when investigating the root cause of negative healthcare incidents: although problems may be rooted in twenty issues, the twenty issues do not cause equal or proportional harm. That is, the top few issues may account for the large majority of problems that cause negative incidents in the hospital. Even more amazing, if the top few problems are properly addressed and resolved, some of the lower-ranking problems will partially or fully disappear as well. Similarly, the borderline may be able to identify twenty people or situations that cause him anxiety that he wishes to avoid. However, *understood proportionally and by priority, there are probably only two or three people or situations that cause the large majority of serious anxiety to the borderline, and avoiding these will attend to the large majority of his anxiety.* This is not to say that the borderline won't experience anxiety when encountering number twelve or fifteen, but twelve and fifteen will produce far less anxiety when numbers one, two, and/or three are eliminated.

This technique serves another purpose. The borderline may catastrophize—that is, feel that the world is always about to explode (or implode) when problems arise. Some problems are more serious than others and this technique will help the borderline compare and contrast the seriousness (or lack of seriousness) of different issues. Over time, the borderline may even see number eighteen, nineteen, or twenty as so obtuse and nonthreatening that some of the items on the list may simply fall out of the borderline's purview and catastrophizing is thus lessened. Finally, *prioritizing the seriousness of problems in this way may also help the borderline better focus on his core values, as it helps him identify what is most important in his life.*

The list of issues can be reviewed and revised every year or two. For example, the borderline may find that a new coworker really pushes his buttons to the extent that the borderline finds himself calling in sick or underperforming at the office. Contending with and identifying the new coworker as a problem may suddenly become a far greater priority than other seemingly important matters near the top of the list because the borderline loves his job and wants to maintain his professional career track.

When I started doing forensic evaluations, many clients would not show up for appointments. This caused me to feel anger and frustration, and I was concerned that my negative feelings prohibited me from properly working with the clients because I had wasted so much time and money (especially as I was renting space by the hour). I developed a list of problems associated with this, but the number one problem was quite simply that the client would not show up, often without reason. I finally came up with a solution that took care of almost everything. I insisted on a nonrefundable deposit with a signed agreement to ensure the client had incentive to show up. Miraculously the clients' nonrefundable deposits eliminated the problem virtually overnight and almost all the other problems associated with this issue. It allowed me to be more in control, predict my schedule, minimize economic loss, and it afforded me much greater certainty as to how much time I would need for a particular case. More importantly, when a client honored his agreement by showing up on time, I felt more relaxed and positively focused on understanding the case. Interestingly, it took me several years to institute this policy because I feared that clients would not give a nonrefundable deposit and seek help elsewhere. What I learned was that clients were essentially in total control and I had no control of my practice prior to instituting the nonrefundable deposit. It was important to reestablish balance so that there was predictability for both the client and myself with regard to cost, scheduling, and expectations so that the client could be responsible for his role and I could be responsible in my professional capacity.

It is also crucial to understand that problems cannot be

solved unless they are first properly identified. We live in an era where it is not politically correct to speak openly about how certain people, cultures, or behaviors may be negative or destructive in various ways. Culture can be positive and beautiful, but culture can also be negative and even ugly. I have interviewed many people who've grown up in drug-filled cultures both within their family and general community. It's a horrible culture to grow up in, although asserting so publicly could be considered ethnically or culturally insensitive. The problem is that in failing to discuss these issues it is impossible to identify where the real problems lie and therefore impossible to attend to the problem on the individual or community level. In fact, *if the borderline cannot properly identify problems, then very often problems are misidentified and something else or someone else is blamed because that other target is less threatening or a politically correct object of scorn.* For this reason, intuitive reasoning is insufficient.

Avoid the Intuitive

If I'm not for me then who will be for me? And when I am alone, what am I? And If not now, then when?
> – *Pirkei Avot*, 1:14

Daniel Kahneman, a Nobel laureate in economics who never actually took an economics course, and Amos Tversky, found that judgment and decisions are often based on bias, prejudice, and false assumptions that ultimately prohibit even professionals from acting in a manner consistent with the best practices of the profession. They reshaped the psychology of human judgment by proposing that instead of dependency on complex systems, we in fact only use a limited number of simple cognitive short hands, or heuristics, when presented with limited outside information. While it may be easier to make good judgments if all pertinent information is available many of the decisions we make in every-day life are made without such advantages. When faced with a knowledge-poor situation or under constraints of time or uncertainty, we instead depend on rules of thumb or intuitive cognitive heuristics. Thus, people tend to be overconfident about their understanding of problems, which can cause them to overestimate their knowledge, underestimate risks, and exaggerate their ability to control events.

Kahneman asserts that there are two kinds of thinking. "System one" entails quick, automatic, intuitive responses often in dire situations when fight or flight responses are needed while "system two" thinking helps to regulate system one, as it relies on slow deliberative rational thinking and judgment which requires effort, time, and energy. The large majority of our decisions are system one in nature. Kahneman argues that both are required for sound judgment and that system one and two complement one another to the thinker's benefit. While system one entails a knee-jerk reaction system two is deliberative and reflective—and motivates us towards better understanding.

As such, decisions are based at least in part on emotions, and not rationality. The reality is that our decisions, proclivities, interests, likes and dislikes—and even biases and prejudices—are ultimately based on a calculus rooted in psychological and emotional underpinnings (such as fear, sadness, anger, resentment, anxiety, and even retaliation), which we then rationalize as reasonable (or even logical) based on a perceived fact pattern and our present and past experiences. For this reason, it is extremely important to be self-aware of emotions—and egos—recognizing whether a decision is rooted in sound judgment or a judgment rooted in emotions that may be irrational, dangerous, or even self-destructive.

An important lesson can be learned from diets. Why don't people lose weight on diets? The reason is that people look at themselves in the mirror and estimate how much they need to lose—say ten pounds. The person then loses five pounds and thinks: well I'm halfway there, great job. The problem is that the original goal of ten pounds is a gross underestimate of how much weight the person really needs to lose. Most people who think they need to lose ten pounds really need to lose significantly more. Losing five pounds makes you feel like you're halfway there though in reality the initial weight loss is almost all water and only a fraction of what needs to be lost to get to the ideal body weight. As such, the initial estimate is wrong based on a poor intuitive guess. In general, diet plans are probably good in that they focus on lower caloric intake, a balanced diet, and many have food recipes to help with the struggle. The reason that diet plans don't work is because people don't follow them. After a few weeks or even months, the person becomes tired of the diet plan or might even feel that because he lost five or ten pounds that he has made sufficient progress physically and even psychologically that he can veer away from the diet plan. A similar phenomenon occurs with self-help books. A person buys a self-help book; they may read it cover to cover and may even make changes that improve the quality of their life. The problem is that the self-help book is not adhered to long-term. After a couple weeks or months, the person then buys another self-help book, again gains personal insight and even enjoys personal growth, but soon enough puts down the book and returns to his intuitive sense of how to live, which may even be self-destructive. *Long-term positive gain is only possible through long-term consistent adherence to proper guidelines and professional supports because the borderline's intuition is often error-prone, underestimating the seriousness of particular issues or how to go about effectively tackling the issues.* A good counterbalance to the intuitive is professional books.

Read Professional Books

> I am thinking therefore I am.
> – Anonymous

> Books are a great disguise.
> – Anonymous

> Wisdom does not come from growing older but from education and learning.
> – Anton Chekhov

Education can provide transformative behavior, emotion, and thinking (though medications do not work better when the person understands the pharmacology of the drug). Researching and reading about medical issues can be challenging because the language may be inaccessible and scientific research methodology incomprehensible. However, this is less so for psychiatric issues. People with psychiatric problems—including BPD—are encouraged to read books by mental health professionals because they are generally readable even if you have to dip into a dictionary now and again (as I do). I was recently rereading some early books on borderlines and I was struck by how instructive these books were not just for someone who understands the subject but for anyone with BPD. There is a great advantage to reading about BPD from professional books rather than just highlights from the Internet. For many years I did not read long history books, but when COVID-19 hit I had more free time because work was slow and synagogue was closed. So I read big biographies of all of the U.S. Presidents from George Washington to Ulysses S. Grant. I previously read many articles on these Presidents but reading a long-sustained tome provided an in-depth understanding that would not otherwise have been possible. Similarly, borderlines should make the effort to read professional books and slowly absorb the information to gain a better understanding of their issues. *For borderlines, knowledge is power and professional books have case vignettes to illustrate how particular clinical issues affect borderlines in their everyday lives. This allows for the integration of theory with practice with the possibility of real solutions.*

Solution-Focused Therapy

We need not be responsible for the world that created our minds, but we can take responsibility for the mind with which we create our world.

— Gabor Maté

Searching the Internet will yield information about a wide range of therapy options for BPD, and indeed for almost anybody with any problem, including dialectical behavior therapy and mindfulness training. There are numerous other nonpharmacological treatments, including simple rest, music therapy, biofeedback, acupuncture, tai chi, yoga, and deep breathing, which allows for a non-psychological connection between the conscious and unconscious. However, *solution-focused therapy is something that borderlines do not usually come across on Internet searches although it can be quite helpful, as it focuses on incremental positive steps, future-oriented goals, strengths rather than weaknesses, and coping strategies rather than problems.*

Solution-focused therapy has several parts. The first part is the miracle question which asks the person to visualize what it would be like waking up tomorrow if the problem were no longer a problem. Some borderlines can never imagine things getting better, so the miracle question gives the borderline permission to fantasize about a normal life. (Generally, fantasy helps us to consider unconscious motivations—often our true passions—that we do not say out loud because it is shameful or simply too hard to articulate). Second, the coping question asks what is the most positive or helpful thing that has lessened symptoms. This allows the borderline to identify an inner strength and build on it as a basis for healthy functioning. The third question asks the person to identify when the problem or symptom does not exist. Being able to identify the context when symptoms are absent or less severe can be quite helpful. Lastly, the person is asked to consider the severity of particular symptoms and how a level 8 problem can be lowered to a level 7 problem. Lowering the symptom just one level can be extremely helpful with the possibility of lowering symptoms even one step further.

Another lesser-known modality is Nonviolent Communication in which an observation is made, perhaps about the environment, a feeling statement is attached, and then translated as a human need with a request to help attend to the feeling in a manner that allows for increased clarity and empathy while avoiding interpersonal conflict.

Counterfactual thinking is a cousin to solution-focused therapy, and it helps develop a capacity for realistic self-criticism and even end vicious cycles of harmful behavior. Borderlines sometimes suffer from regret ("I should have done something different") and self-criticism ("you idiot"). Counterfactual thinking is a future-oriented thought experiment imagining a different future. You have to imagine—or pretend—different scenarios and then work out what could happen next. Imagining a different future and thinking about alternate possibilities and outcomes allows the borderline to de-focus from the stress of this moment and consider positive possibilities in the next moment. However, sometimes the single most focused solution to a problem is removing yourself permanently from the problem.

Abandon Toxicity

One of the first things that a child learns in a healthy family is trust.
> – Mr. Rogers, Senate Hearing, 1969

Now the wind has changed direction and I have to leave.
> – Bernie Taupin, *Border Song*

A masterly retreat is itself a victory.
> – Norman Vincent Peale

No matter where I lived, geography could not save me.
> – Isabel Wilkerson

The borderline may feel that criticism and negativity disproportionately weigh heavily on him, perhaps because borderlines are hypersensitive so that even slight criticisms or negativity feel like a burning character assassination. *The borderline should ask himself a simple question: Is this person going to make me feel better about myself or worse? If the answer is worse, stay away from that person—even if means staying away from close family members.* (On the ABC show *The Goldbergs*, there is an ongoing struggle between the mother and father about competing philosophies on child-rearing. The father believes that children must be told of their limitations and the cruelty of the world that they're going to face as adults, while the mother asserts that there will be a lifetime of people to put down their children so that her job is to convince them that they're wonderful, loved, and very capable. Obviously, both parents are correct. Just as negativity and criticism can destroy self-esteem, unearned flattery falsely boosts the ego in an equally destructive manner.) If you want criticism and negativity, get a therapist. That is, *allow criticism and negativity to emerge*

in a safe, caring, clinically-informed, and constructive atmo-
sphere with balanced feedback where there are set boundaries
and understanding between you and the other person.

If the borderline cannot feel trust and enjoy health and safety with his family or community, then he should leave and not return, especially if the borderline has suffered disloyalty and betrayal in these relationships. (Although emotional pain may seem internal it may actually be environmentally based or even place-specific). We put down bad books and dump crazy girlfriends or boyfriends in a heartbeat, but *family and environment remain dangers we tolerate because of familiarity and loyalty, creating a mistaken allegiance to stay in the midst of suffering.* Clearly, even physical distance doesn't mean that there aren't remnants of the harm and memories may haunt the borderline so that even physical departure is not always sufficient for recovery or safety. For some borderlines even a single visit for the holidays, though well-intentioned, can trigger very negative memories as they recall dysfunctional childhoods in a toxic environment.

Few people leave toxic environments, especially if they grow up in a toxic family or community. When your room fills with smoke, you get out. Period. All other considerations suddenly become unimportant. While we have an instinct to flee from danger, we have the opposite inclination when it comes to family and familiar environments. (Asylum cases are based on the assertion that the person has a well-founded fear of harm, causing the person to leave his home and never return.) For many people this will mean not only psychological distance from the toxic environment but also physical distance so that some people may have to leave not only the home, but the city or even the state. Sometimes people do not have the psychological, physical, or financial resources to leave their family or community, or they feel that they must remain because others are dependent on them. This may occur with older children who cannot leave because they provide crucial care for younger siblings and perhaps even for a parent who is the victim of abuse, struggling financially, or abusing drugs.

In the sitcom *Seinfeld*, George Costanza tells Jerry that he has failed at everything he has ever tried, so Jerry suggests that if everything he ever did was wrong then doing the opposite should work. So George goes up to a beautiful woman and tells her outright that he is short, bald, and unemployed—and amazingly she's immediately attracted to him presumably because of his honesty. Environments and families are the same way. If everything about them is unhealthy, then living in the absence of them should be very helpful in leading a safer and healthier life.

Quell Impulsivity

Never run for a bus, there will always be another one.
– Mel Brooks, *The 2000 Year Old Man*

Shallow breathing leads to shallower thinking.
– Kendall Ronin

Marijuana, alcohol, and most other drugs harm key parts of the (developing) brain, including those involved with memory, learning, attention, judgment, coordination, and reaction time. It is impossible to self-regulate when the brain is flooded with negative feelings and thoughts so intense that it leads to mental breakdown, including dissociation, which is similar to psychosis, temporarily or permanently cutting the person off from reality and meaningful thinking and behavior. There are better ways to self-medicate.

You can hack your brain in various ways, including by slowing things down through trance-like activities to help delay impulsive gratification. One of the best strategies is reading for several hours, focusing on long narratives and empathizing with characters, particularly well-written novels or history books. (If lies did not produce truth, we would have no need for fiction). Long reading sessions not only focus the mind but hold the body in a single place—preferably a comfortable chair—allowing for physical relaxation. Another excellent strategy is prolonged physical exercise, such as swimming laps because it forces the body into repeated thoughtless movements. *Exercise reduces stress and allows the body feedback information, confirming that you're alive and capable of self-direction and tolerating controlled pain and stress.* How the brain conceptualizes the world prepares how the body will contend with external realities and perceived threats. If you can change your brain's predictions—and allow for the possibility of error—physical functioning will alter as well, allowing for greater calm and less fear and impulsivity, and better overall decisions will follow.

Exhaustion, which occurs after physical exertion, paradoxically permits full physical (and cognitive) relaxation, thus diminishing impulsivity. People who enjoy physical exhaustion—with appropriate time to recover—tend to experience less anxiety. Writing and brushing teeth with the nondominant hand can also be helpful in decreasing impulsivity, though most people soon give up. Behaviors such as martial arts tend to tap into unhealthy impulsivity even though there are obvious important meditative and self-control aspects involved in martial arts. Some people confuse impulsivity with energy, believing that if someone's energy is depleted, that impulsivity will also lessen. Although there is clearly a link between impulsivity and energy, they are not the same phenomenon, and the way to quell one is not the way to quell the other. *Quelling impulsivity through trance-like activities, such as deep thought, chanting, and even uttering prayers, allows for less self-centered thinking, better external awareness, and greater empathy allowing for a change in perspective.*

Change Perspective

Man is born broken. He lives by mending. The grace of God is glue.
  – Eugene O'Neill

Learning something new means abandoning something that you already knew.
  – Anonymous

The borderline may find that after years or even decades of perceiving relationships and situations in a particular way, a complete change of perspective is needed to alter his perception of reality, and spirituality and mindfulness are great in this regard. Spirituality is one way to change perspective, as it concerns the personal search for meaning outside of our physical and psychological selves, allowing for external connection and imbuing meaning into it. Mindfulness—a healthy form of distraction—concerns maintaining an immediate and moment-by-moment awareness of one's self and surroundings without self-judgment. *However, to be effective, spirituality and mindfulness need self-compassion or else the changed perspective will remain an empty experience.*

Both can facilitate emotional processing and allow for formerly aversive or anxiety-provoking behavior, emotion, and thinking to be considered in the moment. It may also allow the borderline to develop an observing-ego, decentering from his self-centered and tunneled thinking. Perhaps the best change in perspective occurs through feedback from others (including in group therapy). *For the borderline everything seems urgent, immediate, and miserable, so that time is the enemy. The borderline needs to develop the capacity to sit with uncertainty and consider what is external to him as a first step toward self-healing and abandoning the misery of feeling miserable.*

Heal Thyself, Doctor

Let us sing as we go. The road will be less tedious.
   – Virgil Eclogues, Book IX

You've got to be miserable. You don't like yourself. But you do admire yourself. It's all you've got so you cling to it. You're afraid if you change you will lose what makes you special. Being miserable doesn't make you better than anybody else. It just makes you miserable.
   – *House*, S2:E11

My favorite example of a borderline character in pop culture is Dr. Gregory House on the hit Fox TV show *House*. (My favorite movie about a borderline is *The Cable Guy*.) Dr. House is a well-known infectious disease and kidney specialist who takes on challenging cases solving impossible medical mysteries. He abhors people but adopts these cases because he loves puzzles and every human body is basically a mechanical mystery or a moist robot. (If humans are moist robots then perhaps God is a dry human). House has many assets including his high intelligence, a well-respected career with good remuneration, and a best friend who is loyal to a fault (his Dr. Watson).

Dr. House suffers from chronic pain syndrome due to a leg injury caused by an infarction that went undiagnosed for three days until he diagnosed it himself. Dr. House is miserable, and it is heart-wrenching to watch him contend with his physical and psychological pain, loneliness, and how he sabotages his life in various ways year after year. In fact, he abuses various drugs (mostly analgesics but others as well), has an erratic mood and unstable behaviors, burns through personal and professional relationships, and, while perceptive, has poor insight into his own issues, though he does recognize his desultory situation to some extent and later in the series refers to himself as "the most miserable person in the world." It is painful to watch but also very instructive, as the series is a riff on the adage "physician heal thyself." There is a very good episode where a psychopath challenges Dr. House to consider if he isn't also a psychopath given his complete disdain for other people, suggesting for the first time in the series the possibility of a psychiatric diagnosis (or differential diagnosis).

There are several interesting aspects to Dr. House. First, he's completely misdiagnosed. He is seen as a drug-addicted narcissist, but BPD is never once mentioned in the series even though he's surrounded by doctors, including psychiatrists, in a premier medical center. Second, Dr. House suffers from unbearable physical and psychological pain. Neither is adequately addressed through pharmaceuticals or otherwise. *Dr. House is misunderstood, misdiagnosed, and mistreated. Sound familiar?*

Many borderlines probably recognize that their psychiatric and personal issues have not been properly identified or misunderstood by healthcare professionals, including their primary care physician who has known the person for many years. Dr. House does a lousy job diagnosing himself and self-medicating, however, the sad truth is that the healthcare experts who surround him are no better at pinpointing his problems and therefore Dr. House's unconventional methods of attending to his symptoms may ultimately be necessary because no one else seems to truly understand him.

What's particularly interesting is that Dr. House is an open book and never holds back voicing his thoughts or feelings, no matter how inappropriate so that the doctors who surround Dr. House do not have to guess what he's feeling or thinking and his impulsive behaviors are also available for everyone to see—and yet Dr. House remains undiagnosed and very ill. As such, *self-advocacy and even self-treatment may sometimes be appropriate and even necessary when after years of being surrounded by healthcare professionals little progress is made.*

Anticipate Positive Change as You Age

> The research literature has identified three factors that universally lead to stress: uncertainty, lack of information, and loss of control.
>
> – Gabor Maté

The diagnosis of BPD as a young adult can be quite difficult to accept. (The borderline probably had various behavior, emotion, and thinking problems that his pediatrician ignored. In the last twenty years the vast majority of children I've seen with mental health issues were ignored by their pediatricians). For eons (or at least decades) it was assumed that development was something unique to children, though we now understand that development—physical, psychological, and otherwise—occurs throughout the life-span and well into our geriatric years, and even dying has stages. The good news is that many mental health problems tend to decrease over time or become more manageable as symptoms become less severe.

It's not unusual for a borderline to gaze back at his behavior, emotion, or thinking with credulity, finding that the anger harbored in early adulthood seems irrelevant decades later, impulsive risky sexual behavior somehow later seems foolish, and the insecurity of attachment is replaced by the love of a few close relationships, allowing for a sense of solace that the borderline never before enjoyed. While it is important to regard BPD seriously it is also crucial to revisit the diagnosis and symptoms now and again to consider what does and does not remain true and relevant. *While it is true that new or different symptoms can develop, particularly in reaction to life stressors, it is equally true that personal growth, development, and maturity can counteract or even eliminate certain symptoms.* New stressors rarely fully set back the borderline to square one and weathering storms seem to be less challenging as the borderline ages. It is also not uncommon for borderlines to experience the remission of a concomitant diagnosis such as depression, an eating disorder, or substance abuse.

Borderlines who find a new career may discover that it allows for frustration and anxiety to lessen. The new job may be a completely new opportunity in life not only to develop a fresh professional career but to work in an environment with competent colleagues and on projects that are personally satisfying. The other major switch is that some borderlines give up on a string of Ms. Wrongs and finally consider Ms. Right. Why this change occurs is not exactly clear, but a lifelong commitment based on legitimate trust and love with a supportive partner who understands the borderline's psychiatric issues can be a truly life-changing event. *Because everyone changes and develops, it's important to have someone who understands the clinical aspects of the borderline's life and for this reason sticking with therapy long-term can be extremely helpful.*

Stay In Therapy Even If It's Dull

Someone has to say to you: I believe in your ability to recover, to have a better life, and I am going to stick with you until you do.
    – Jay Neugeboren

If two people are in therapy it helps if one of them isn't anxious.
    – Molyn Leszcz

What frightens us today is exactly the same sort of thing that frightened us yesterday. It's just a different wolf.
    – Alfred Hitchcock

When I share my fear and shame it seems to lessen or maybe the fear and shame just has less power over me when it's not just swirling around in my head.
    – Anonymous

To wrestle with your demons will cause your angels to sing.
    – August Wilson

Therapy can assist the borderline in myriad ways with short-term and long-term positive benefits. Because the borderline develops during adulthood, he needs someone who understands *clinically* how change affects him and thus help guide him when he comes to a fork in the road. Obviously, it's important to find the right therapist, and with the right modality, so that the borderline can establish a sense of trust or therapeutic alliance and realistic goals. Therapeutic goals are not always hugely important, as the focus of therapy is the therapeutic alliance itself and the corrective emotional experience. People benefit from therapy in different ways over a period of months or years and many people, including borderlines, benefit in ways that they do not even realize. Therapy may seem dull because several core issues are talked about repeatedly sometimes making therapy seem ineffective. However, it is the very return to core issues thinking and rethinking them from different emotional vantage points that may be most helpful. *Although progress may not be linear, staying in therapy is crucial regardless of whether the borderline believes it helps because therapy is a professional holding environment where a clinical expert can provide support and feedback in ways that are simply impossible in any other context or relationship.*

It's not unusual for borderlines to feel that they are ignored, misunderstood, or even ridiculed by others. As such, it is not unusual for the borderline to go from therapist to therapist disappointed that he has not found someone who understands him. Obviously, the borderline needs to be with a therapist he feels comfortable with so that a therapeutic alliance of trust is possible. However, the therapist is not a friend, but a clinical service provider. There is something beneficial about giving a therapist (or any professional) the benefit of the doubt just like you give your doctor the benefit of the doubt (even given the huge number of medical errors in medicine).

Regular visits to a psychiatrist for medication may or may not be helpful, but these visits occur only every few months and amount to little more than saying hello and getting a new prescription. Weirdly, in the United States, the majority of psychiatric medication is prescribed by non-psychiatrists, such as primary care physicians, who have minimal expertise in clinical mental health. (In 1954, antipsychotic medications emerged, permitting some persons afflicted with schizophrenia to experience an almost miraculous decrease in hallucinations, delusions, and even negative symptoms. In turn, psychiatrists came to assume that medications could cure all psychiatric illnesses or at least decrease symptoms to a remarkable degree. However, psychiatry has taken this to an extreme and, with the massive influence of Big Pharma, the large majority of psychiatrists only prescribe medication and the vast majority of psychotherapy is conducted by non-psychiatrists). *Medications can be extremely helpful for a wide variety of reasons, but talk therapy is priceless beyond jewels.*

The borderline should also stay in therapy for his present or future partner. The borderline may find himself content now, but in a few months or years he will find himself in a relationship. Even if that relationship is healthy and safe, the borderline may inexplicably find himself at times acutely angry, frustrated, or even lashing out at his partner for whom he feels genuine love. Thus, *therapy not only attends to past injuries and present situations, but it also helps with issues that will emerge in future relationships in unanticipated ways. The borderline must plan with both short-term and long-term strategies to live a meaningful and content life for himself and his loved ones.*

While there is a saturation of psychotherapists in places such as New York and Los Angeles, there is a drought of mental health professionals in many other parts of the United States. For many people, psychiatric care is anathema to their cultural background and mental health diagnoses are stigmatized. For the borderline who grew up in such a place it may be hard to connect with a therapist, but the effort must still be made.

In therapy, thoughts and feelings are processed to understand where they come from, how they affect us, and how we can live our lives in a more constructive manner. In reality, however, some thoughts and feelings are best left in the basement or attic (we live in an apartment so I don't know from either) because contending with these thoughts and feelings will not necessarily be helpful or yield positive psychological growth, especially for high-functioning people. My father was once referred a patient for consultation because the physician thought that the patient could benefit from therapy. My father assessed the patient and wrote back to the physician: "leave well enough alone." Sometimes no therapy is a better option, especially if the person benefits from other sources of support and insight, such as an executive functioning helper.

Get an Executive Director or Co-Manager

Another flaw in the human character is that everybody wants to build and nobody wants to do maintenance.
 – Kurt Vonnegut, *Hocus Pocus*

Mann Tracht, Un Got Lacht (Man Makes Plans and God Laughs)
 – Yiddish Proverb

Almost anyone with serious cognitive deterioration is aware that an executive director or co-manager is a crucial support to ensure continued independence and personal dignity. Just like a person with dementia benefits from someone helping with decisions while he is still relatively cognitively intact, the borderline should also consider an executive director or co-manager proactively rather than when he finds himself in a position where he is struggling financially and in every other way, just barely surviving or perhaps even on the brink of homelessness. Sometimes more than one executive helper is needed.

Indeed, athletes don't have one coach but many coaches. *Do not leave all the power in your own hands because it will lead to self-cruelty.*

Executive coaches also help with conditioning and discipline, and provide honest feedback when the person is headed in the wrong direction or driven towards failure. Most importantly, an executive coach will help you emulate how persons who contend with similar obstacles surmount their issues, often through repetitive dedication to specific strategies and surpassing their own expectations.

The borderline does not have to abandon his freedom to make decisions by having someone look over his shoulder or second-guess his every move, but rather it can be very helpful to have someone with whom he can think through decisions thoughtfully and constructively. This will allow the borderline to feel more secure in his daily organization and quell problems with disorganization, impulsivity, and even emotional dysregulation. *It can be difficult for a young adult to have to admit that his decisions are sufficiently poor that he needs supervision to help manage everyday issues and yet the ability to recognize when help is needed and in what form is among the best indicators that a person will remain safe and healthy.*

Ideas from AA

Habit is habit, and not to be flung out of the window by any man, but coaxed downstairs a step at a time.
- Mark Twain, *Pudd'nhead Wilson*

Alcoholics Anonymous has many therapeutic aspects in its twelve-step program; among the most beneficial is the sponsor. A sponsor is a nonclinical expert who is also a recovering alcoholic who provides nonjudgmental support to the alcoholic at any time regardless of the issue. The alcoholic may be sober for several months, have a drink, and then call the sponsor. The sponsor will respond with open-ended non-critical support, encouraging the alcoholic that it was a bump in the road and that the person is now back on the road to sobriety with better decision-making.

The borderline may have several friends, good clinical care, and even a partner for support, yet many borderlines have supports who simply do not understand the psychopathology of BPD because it is so baffling, counter-intuitive, contradictory, and difficult for an outsider to discern the internal chaotic world of the borderline. *For alcoholics, finding a sponsor is relatively easy because there are AA meetings seemingly everywhere and recovering alcoholics understand alcoholism as a chronic and incurable disease. Finding a BPD sponsor is more of a challenge, but the benefits are enormous.*

Another positive aspect of AA is the idea that an alcoholic can declare that he is sober at any time by abstaining from alcohol even for one day. The borderline may also find himself making endless declarations such as "I'm on a diet" or "I'm done with clubbing," which seem terribly disingenuous and unhelpful. However, such declarations are in fact very helpful for borderlines, allowing the person a new start at any moment, even if a relapse occurs the day after the declaration. The more often the declarations are made, the more likely it is the borderline will consider maintaining it as a new normal for longer periods. Additionally, the spoken verbal declaration itself is a positive recognition of the pathology, which is always the first step toward healing and recovery. *In AA, sobriety is not achieved, it is declared.*

There are, however, drawbacks to the Alcoholics Anonymous model. The model does not consider individual clinical issues or the etiology of a person's problems. It treats all alcoholics as having the same problem and therefore every alcoholic can, in theory, benefit from the same solution. The AA members who I have met assume that their inner-child was traumatized causing alcoholism or other psychiatric issues and that their childhood experiences induced them to endure guilt and helplessness. There is also an assumption that all children are innocent, though this is obviously false. However, there are clearly people who suffer with such issues and yet enjoyed a healthy childhood. AA is a life-saving program for countless people and the model has been copied for many other addictions because of the successful core philosophy that people are not bad but rather misunderstood because addiction is a disease.

You Are Not Bad, Just Misunderstood

Personality is a very mysterious thing. A man cannot always be estimated by what he does. He may keep the law and yet be worthless. He may break the law, and yet be fine. He may be bad, without ever doing anything bad. He may commit a sin against society, and yet realize through that sin his own perfection.

– Oscar Wilde

The borderline may believe he is bad or even evil. It is crucial to understand that he is neither bad nor evil. Bad implies purposeful wrongdoing, hurting others without consideration for consequences. Sometimes our genetics or even a medical issue—or virus or bacteria—will make us behave, feel, or think in a certain way that may be harmful to ourselves or others. As noted earlier, *borderlines may act in a hurtful manner, but it is part and parcel of the pathology and they do not act with animus.* That is, the borderline is not a psychopath and he does not have antisocial personality disorder.

I had a client who suffered for many decades from alcohol abuse and also several years of opioid addiction. (Addiction gives us warped warmth). When I saw her she was clean for about a year. She told me about her sad life and her husband was also forthcoming about her history of self-harm. What amazed me, however, was that this woman presented as completely normal without mental health problems. She was a pleasure to speak with, articulate and intelligent, and it became clear that while addicted to alcohol and drugs, she was directed toward injurious behavior completely out of her control. She was not bad or evil but under a harmful influence and when that influence was removed from her mind and body the amazing person that she is soon returned. *The borderline may have to live with being a borderline his whole life due to predetermined genetics or trauma, but the borderline is not defined by genetics or trauma.*

Don't Allow Shame to Humiliate You

> I have lived my whole life in shame. Why should I die with dignity?
> – George Costanza, *Seinfeld*, S4:E23

Among the single most important elements of survival for the borderline is to recognize that he is battling a disease that influences his behavior, emotion, and thinking—and so he has no reason to feel shame, self-incrimination, or guilt about his behavior, emotion, and thinking. Still, shame persists for many borderlines. One very serious problem with borderlines, and in general for people with depression, is that they feel ashamed of being unhappy and they often exhaust themselves trying to establish false positive exteriors to hide that shame. *The unhappiness of shame can be debilitating and it can lead to social withdrawal and lies about who you are.* The borderline should never feel ashamed of who he is and self-acceptance brings him one step closer to reclaiming his humanity.

Grey Days Are Optimal

Children begin by loving their parents. After a time they judge
them. Rarely, if ever, do they forgive them.
> – Oscar Wilde

Things are black and white.
There's right and there's wrong.
It's simple!
Until it isn't anymore.
Then everything is just a shade of grey.
Some more intense than others.
Some more destructive than others.
But, grey.
> – Anonymous

From about 1920 to 1980, psychodynamic theory (also known
as psychoanalytic theory, though there are differences) domi-
nated clinical and intellectual life in the United States, Europe,
and other parts of the world. (Marxism was the other domi-
nant ideology). While psychodynamics offers a wide range of
ideas—and countless counter-ideas—there are a few schools
within psychodynamics that are worth consideration. First,
Id Psychology asserts that people are driven by instinctual
drives toward sex and death. Second, Ego Psychology asserts
that the ego mediates different parts of the psyche and helps
defend against negative thoughts and feelings. These ideas
are somewhat well-known in popular culture. However, there
was a third major development called Object Relations. Object
Relations theory asserts that as a child grows, he develops his
identity and positive or negative sense of self—and even his values—through relationships with primary caregivers. The child
initially idealizes the caregiver as wonderful and loving, though
through maturation the child learns to his dismay that just as
he is far from perfect, his caregivers are also quite human with
negative aspects as well as positive aspects to their identity.

The healthy adult is able to integrate and balance these different images and ideas of self and other without anger or resentment, allowing for love of self and other—and understanding and forgiveness.

Object Relations theory is helpful because borderlines tend to demonize or idealize other people, conceptualizing them as all good or all bad when in fact mature relationships can only occur when we understand that our imperfections define us. The borderline may be very demanding with a strong sense of entitlement, belittling the other person with degrading verbal and other psychological abuses, or the borderline may interact in a docile manner, perhaps idealizing the other person, deferring to his judgment and even his value system.

Strive to see grey and nuance without judgment or criticism for at least a few moments when meeting someone—be it a teacher, family member, or even a waiter in a restaurant when all you want to do is scarf down a greasy burger. Allow the person's image, behavior, and idiosyncrasies to affect you for a few moments while his presence settles into your mind before impulsive assumptions set in. *Seeing grey does not mean becoming dull; it means re-owning nuance and understanding conflict without anger and even good humor—and thinking before acting.*

Sleep

I'm not just tired I'm physically exhausted all the time. Being a borderline zaps my energy.

– Anonymous

Innocent sleep. Sleep that soothes away all our worries. Sleep that puts each day to rest. Sleep that relives the weary laborer and heals hurt minds. Sleep, the main course in life's feast, and the most nourishing.

– William Shakespeare, *Macbeth*

Cognitive dysfunction or dysregulation is almost impossible to contend with without professional help. However, even established therapies may require weeks or months until positive results emerge. Even then, cognitive dysfunction in various forms may continue because altering how information is processed can be extremely challenging. However, there is one thing that can be done to literally shut off the brain—a good night's sleep. Sleep is extremely healthy and reiterating the myriad benefits of sleep, including battling general cognitive decline, is unnecessary here. Sleep in the cold, total darkness (eye blinders are excellent), with no distractions, in a bed where you do nothing but sleep with comfortable and inviting sheets, blankets, and pillows, and prepare for sleep with rituals that help promote physical and mental exhaustion, including reading for one hour before bed. *Sleep remains the only true method of cutting through cognitive dysfunction while also allowing the brain to process (and possibly make sense of) information absorbed during the day—and this may also help diminish psychic pain.* It is not unusual for borderlines who endure severe psychological pain to wake up almost having forgotten that the psychological pain ever existed until various cues kick in, reminding him of the reality that a new day has dawned and, sadly, life is very much the same.

Trust Your Body and Your Doctor

Your brain keeps the score, but your body is the scorecard.
    – Lisa Feldman Barrett

Now do you believe me? You bastards!
    – What's written on the hypochondriac's tombstone

Even a broken clock must be right twice a day.
    – Anonymous

The borderline often harbors self-doubt, questioning his judgment and distrusting his feelings. Similarly, the borderline may distrust his own body—at times acting paranoid as if the body is out to get him or undermine his ability to enjoy life. Borderlines are constantly fighting unwelcome or unpleasant thoughts and feelings, but also body pain or discomfort. Borderlines, as noted earlier in the book, tend to have multiple physical complaints or somatic issues, particularly regarding gastrointestinal discomfort, headaches or migraines, general aches and pains, and complaints of fatigue or low energy, feeling unable to face the challenges of everyday life. For this reason, I always ask clients, "How does your body react to anxiety and stress?" *Stress can be psychologically and also physically toxic.*

The mind-body debate ended decades ago when it became clear that the brain is an organ within the body so that all thoughts and ideas occur within the body. It is a single unit of multiple inter-functioning and inter-influencing systems, all of which have a neurophysiological impact on behavior, emotion, and thinking. So it makes sense that when your arm hurts you feel psychic pain because of the neuromuscular system and so too when you feel anxious your arm may hurt because of the same feedback system.

If the borderline can develop a language for his body pain (physiological distress), it may help stop the internalization of psychological pain and this, in turn, can help destroy the façade of inauthenticity. Art therapy can be helpful because it allows unadulterated internal issues to be expressed in art form, externally. The goal is to reduce stress in the body, as much as to reduce psychological stress, allowing the body's regulatory system to become accessible and function unhindered. (In general, it is important for the borderline to separate the symptoms that comprise BPD from his personal humanity because without humanization the individual is swallowed up by the illness).

The borderline who believes he has a medical issue should seek a medical opinion. However, if the doctor determines there is no medical issue then there is no medical issue. It is important that the borderline does not become his own doctor and second-guess medical opinions or live in fear and anxiety because of Internet information. Yet, there are several important caveats to this. First, medical error is not uncommon in the United States and seeking a second or third opinion is crucial. Second, revisiting the problem if it does not resolve may also be wise. Third, Internet information can indeed be very informative and sometimes provide options that doctors do not. I had a very painful foot issue and doctors suggested various over-the-counter and prescription medications, some of which were expensive and had various degrees of effectiveness. I chanced upon curcumin as an anti-inflammatory agent, which yielded better results than anything prescribed or suggested by physicians and it is cheap, has no side effects, and can be taken with any meal any time of the day. There is scientific research supporting the use of curcumin, yet the reason doctors do not suggest it is because Big Pharma has an oversized influence on medical practice to the detriment of patients and the entire healthcare system. *Overall, the body has a science-fiction-like capacity to heal and maintain homeostasis under normal circumstances, and constantly second-guessing how the body functions and whether it is functioning properly is unhelpful, so that deference to physicians who know better is often the best path for borderlines.*

The Silver Lining

Hope is the thing with feathers.
    – Emily Dickson

Healthcare problems can be broken down into various categories, including chronic, acute, and emergency. However, chronic issues may have periods of relative calm so that even cancer can enter a period of remission. *Hope is crucial for the border-line, believing that with proper support and time he will enjoy a renewed sense of well-being.* (According to Hesiod, Hope is the only virtue that Pandora did not allow to escape from the jar). The problem, however, is that the borderline suffering from psychological pain gains little or no comfort when told that pain will diminish given enough time. I have had pain because of different medical issues over the years. The most fascinating aspect of pain is that when there is horrible pain, which sometimes lasts for several days, it is difficult to re-member enjoying life without pain. Similarly, when feeling perfectly healthy biking a hundred miles a week, I cannot recall the physical or psychological feeling of pain. Moreover, I must confess that when I'm feeling great, pain seems so foreign that when a client talks about his pain it can be challenging to relate to his suffering, aside from clinical sympathy. Without hope the borderline has nothing and if he has nothing he is left only with pain.

Symptoms are complicated, especially because they appear differently in different people with different degrees of seri-ousness. For example, insomnia is a widely noted symptom in several psychiatric diagnoses and it can also exist as a problem in its own right (primary insomnia). But insomnia affects differ-ent people differently. A writer who lives alone may find that his most productive hours for writing occur late into the night. For the writer, the insomnia is ego-syntonic, that is, the insom-nia is in harmony with his professional and personal needs. In contrast, a father who has to be awake and alert, arriving at a factory every day at 8 AM, may find that insomnia prohibits him from rising in the morning or properly functioning at the factory, leading to repeated reprimands or even employment termination so that he can no longer feed his family, making the insomnia ego-dystonic.

While BPD symptoms may seem negative and frightening,

there are ways to consider, interpret, or even utilize the symptoms in a transformative and even positive way. The Hebrew/ Yiddish phrase *"Gum Zo L'Tova"* means "this too is for the best." It suggests that even negative occurrences in life can be interpreted to mean something positive and hopeful. The following are examples relevant to BPD.

Sensitivity to emotional and social cues, especially negative ones. This can be reinterpreted as empathy for the moods and thoughts of others, especially the suffering of others. Because the borderline can be quite sensitive or even hypersensitive to emotional and social cues (and facial expressions) it can cause him to feel uneasy in social situations and even act or react in inappropriate ways. However, a positive way to interpret this is that borderlines have a special capacity for empathy and the needs of others, and are often deep intuitive thinkers.

Impulsivity and reactivity. This can be reinterpreted as spontaneity and excitement. Impulsivity and reactivity may sound negative, though spontaneity and excitement can have positive connotations. There is something very positive about people who can be spontaneous, curious, and create excitement in their own lives and the lives of others as a means to explore new things, people, ideas, and places, including new or unusual restaurants, museums, and much else. Some borderlines lead their lives to the fullest, putting aside a conservative lifestyle and parochial values in favor of *carpe diem.*

Lack of boundaries. This can be reinterpreted as the ability to merge. While most people dip their toe in the water before making connections in new relationships, borderlines may be more willing to jump right in, making connections and meeting new people even while blurring boundaries. This also allows the borderline to fall easily in love and even see things in ways that are new and different from other people while often wishing to share their experiences, thoughts, and feelings.

Intensely emotional can be reinterpreted as passionate and lead to unexpected creativity. A religious borderline who was away from home with his family realized that the family had traveled without prayer books. Deeply missing prayer time, he wrote from memory those prayers that were most meaningful, allowing the family to have something to read for Sunday morning services.

Rage can be reinterpreted as passion. A client often expressed rage at the indifference of large corporations toward the environment. Rather than simply remain angry, he adopted compassion toward the environment and became a lifelong and tireless advocate, making a positive difference that others could emulate.

Vengeful can be reinterpreted as a strong sense of right and wrong. Borderlines who feel slighted may harbor an intense sense of anger seeking revenge, but this can also be understood as the borderline having a strong sense of right and wrong. The valiant knight who wishes to avenge the harmed damsel identifies with the harm she suffers and goes on a selfless quest to avenge her honor.

Fear of abandonment can be reinterpreted as strong personal attachments. Fear of abandonment can also be understood as the borderline enjoying a very strong sense of interpersonal attachment to another person, removing it from the singular self-centered to a dyadic healthy bond.

Neediness can be reinterpreted as a willingness to please. Similar to the fear of abandonment, which is often conceptualized as a self-centered issue, neediness can be reconceptualized as a willingness to please, making a particular effort to ensure that an important relationship remains stable, healthy, and secure.

Unstable sense of self can be reinterpreted as flexibility. By virtue of the borderline's unstable sense of self, it can allow him to be quite flexible in some ways, bending to the needs of others in a sometimes docile and compliant manner.

Boundaries and Compartmentalization

Pretending to care saves me from having to understand.
> – *Pepper and Salt*, WSJ

Do what you can with what you have. Nothing more is needed.
> – Rick Rubin

It's a mistake to classify the passions as lawful and unlawful, so as to yield to the one and refuse the other. All alike are good if we are their masters; all alike are bad if we abandon ourselves to them. Nature forbids us to extend our relations beyond the limits of our strength; reason forbids us to want what we cannot get, conscience forbids us, not to be tempted, but to yield to temptation. To feel or not to feel a passion is beyond our control, but we can control ourselves. Every sentiment under our own control is lawful; those which control us are criminal. A man is not guilty if he loves his neighbor's wife, provided he keeps this unhappy passion under the control of the law of duty; he is guilty if he loves his own wife so greatly as to sacrifice everything to that love.
> – Jean-Jacques Rousseau, *Confessions*, Book V

Borderlines need to compartmentalize not only thoughts and feelings, but also behavior and interpersonal relationships. *Compartmentalizing impulsive or destructive behaviors in private life will allow the borderline to still thrive in various other ways in his public life.* People have a general tendency to want to make friends everywhere and blur boundaries between professional and personal life. This is not only unnecessary but unhealthy for the borderline who may wish to keep parts of his life not only separate but secret, not only to allow his community persona to flourish but for personal self-protection. That is, compartmentalizing hateful thoughts to one section of the borderline's consciousness will allow him to consciously get along in the world in a safer and healthier way. The borderline tends to overshare thoughts and feelings (and even behaviors) when in fact professional development can be hindered when inappropriate personal issues are inserted into the workspace. For example, a serious boundary-crossing situation occurs when the borderline seeks out sexual relationships in inappropriate venues, such as with work supervisors or subordinates, which is not only inappropriate but also potentially professionally devastating. For the borderline it is not only important to understand where he starts and another person stops but also to understand that different conversations and behaviors are appropriate in different contexts and for different reasons. *Eliminating negative or hateful behavior, emotion, and thinking altogether is a laudable goal but often unrealistic and perhaps even unhelpful for the borderline who may benefit more from respecting boundaries and compartmentalization.*

Benefit from the Experience of Others, But Don't Overidentify

I like hearing myself talk. It is one of my greatest pleasures. I often have long conversations all by myself, and I am so clever that sometimes I don't understand a single word of what I am saying.
- Oscar Wilde

Anyone is better than no one.
- Anonymous

> The more we pay attention, the more we begin to realize that all the work we ever do is collaboration.
> – Rick Rubin

People have too much pride to admit that sadness and loneliness deeply effect their behavior, emotion, and thinking. Pride and shame are deadly sins that prevent people from reaching out for help even when it's absolutely needed. For borderlines, pride may even trump self-preservation. (Though guilt accounts for about 80% of our decisions). *People tend to feel less alone when they meet others whose hardships are similar, making life more manageable.* This is why group therapy for borderlines can be very helpful, as gaining feedback from group members can be quite therapeutic. People with BPD have a lot in common with each other given the peculiarity of their symptoms and dysfunction, so much so that BPD groups are a culture unto itself.

While there's a great deal of utter nonsense and even falsehood on the Internet which needs to be weeded out and avoided, there is a fantastic benefit to this availability. The internet offers concise autobiographical insights into people's lives and many people have utilized YouTube to express personal struggles with total honesty. The result is that people with particular disorders or problems can understand and identify with others with similar issues in an immediate way and in a humanistic and honest manner. When I was a student there were basically two ways to understand clinical issues. First, read about people in clinical vignettes. However, these were often snippets of a person's life without greater context. Second, learn about people in a clinical setting. However, this is limited by the particular client population or treatment modality. In contrast, autobiographical videos provide opportunities to consider mental health issues that even a clinician may not otherwise encounter or experience. For example, there are many developmental disorders and intellectual disabilities rooted in hundreds of genetic abnormalities, and many people with these issues have uploaded clinically informative videos. Furthermore, BPD has multiple presentations and multiple autobiographical videos provide very different presentations of BPD, which is not obvious from the DMS5 criteria. *Many of the videos reflect how people have successfully contended with mental health issues while also enjoying life to the fullest and accomplishing personal goals.*

Some borderlines turn to the Internet for both impulsive sexual exploration and also to avoid feelings of loneliness and emptiness, though often the two issues greatly overlap. Connecting with strangers on the Internet is a risky endeavor, but it has allowed those who are isolated—particularly those who were are isolated in their homes because of disability or even the COVID-19 pandemic—to connect with others, lessening loneliness, sometimes with positive results, as it helps borderlines to avoid overidentifying with his own problems. Yet, there are also sometimes very negative results. Internet interpersonal connections can quickly become addictive and the superficial connections may ultimately cause the borderline to experience an even more profound sense of isolation and loneliness. Moreover, social media requires the borderline to compare himself to others based on anonymous judgment, which can be unnerving and damaging. Somewhat paradoxically, the vastness of social media may limit the borderline's creativity and curiosity by steering him to perceived norms, though the borderline must constantly consider new strategies to overcome his challenges. Still, for some borderlines the Internet is a life-saving tool that can afford connections, allowing for feedback and the exchange of ideas about treatment options.

This book is written with the male pronoun for reasons noted in the introduction. However, this book would be amiss without noting that women with BPD must be aware that male predators wish to take advantage of the borderline's impulsive nature and fragile sense of self. This can be particularly a problem when the borderline impulsively seeks solace in the form of sexual intimacy or when sex satisfies the borderline's need for praise, emotional support, or even just platonic chitchat. Borderlines—and their partners—may use one another in harmful ways, leading to STIs and a profound sense of loneliness from repeated experiences of empty intimacy. *Unhealthy impulsivity by its nature tends to negate or mute safety considerations perhaps because impulsive people do not have the capacity or willingness to make the same safety calculation as non-impulsive people.*

Don't Allow Pieces of Yourself to Be Torn from You Because the Scaffolding is Fragile

The definition of a friend is someone you can borrow chairs from for a party and not invite the person to the party.
> – Daniel Silver

They can kill you but they can't eat you.
> – Anonymous

Behind my prison bars I do possess what none can take away.
> – Oscar Wilde

Identity is a composite of who we are based on ethnicity, family, environment, personal strengths and weaknesses, proclivities, physical and healthcare issues, and hopes and dreams (and much more). When a person has a clear understanding of his identity, he also tends to have a clear understanding of his needs, what kind of endeavors to focus on, and which people can best support him (and who to avoid). *When a person's identity is uncertain or fractured, the person will seek out others for support through trial and error to repair and inform his sense of self.*

The borderline may feel that he is not internally cohesive, that is, that his identity and psychological health are somehow incomplete or a disrupted mosaic of tiles that may not even properly fit together no matter how desperately he tries to re-arrange the tiles. Additionally, even when all the tiles fit together into a clear mosaic, it is often the case that the borderline will find that the tiles are not properly glued in place or that they can become easily jostled, causing the picture to become obscured. Thus, the borderline's identity is very fragile to begin with and can be easily disrupted. *Whether the fractured picture was not cohesive to begin with (genetic abnormality) or becomes altered or disfigured (dysfunctional or pathological development), the borderline strives to gain meaning through his identity just like everyone else.* When the borderline senses that other people chip away at his mosaic or remove tiles by demeaning his identity or personal integrity, it can be psychologically and emotionally devastating (as it would be for anyone). There is a single crucial question that every borderline should ask himself about another person (especially in romantic situations): Does he make me feel better or worse about myself? *The borderline may place more value on how other people value him than in how he values himself.*

The borderline, therefore, must be particularly careful with whom he develops relationships. A borderline may easily find himself in a destructive relationship or with a partner who does not really support his needs or have his best interest at heart. These destructive partners may chip away at the borderline's identity and personal integrity, and chipping away at a piece that is seemingly small may cause a destructive ripple effect that can shatter the entire edifice. *Additionally, the borderline may be unable to differentiate between major slights and minor slights so that any slight at all can have a negative cascading effect causing havoc.* Nonetheless, the borderline remains in such relationships because he cannot bear loneliness and does not have the psychological wherewithal—or perhaps physical ability—to provide for his own needs. Additionally, the borderline's dysfunction may be so pervasive that the only people who will tolerate him are other people with similar levels of dysfunction. Still, in the long-run it is probably better for the borderline to err on the side of caution engaging in fewer social connections, pushing away anybody who eats away at his fragile mosaic self. *The borderline should not sacrifice pieces of himself just to let someone else feel more complete or to avoid loneliness, particularly because doing so places a great deal of power and control in the other person.*

There is an important related concept called scaffolding, which are artificial structures of psychological support. It is primarily used in the context of children who suffer with developmental and/or learning disabilities. The idea is to provide a strong platform to support the child so that he gains the tools he needs to properly meet personal, academic, social, and community challenges, gaining self-assurance so that by adulthood the child can be largely independent, no longer dependent on scaffolding to feel secure, safe, and stable. The problem is that the borderline may not begin to recognize his personal challenges until he is a young adult, or even older, and placing proper scaffolding in place in adulthood becomes difficult and sometimes even impossible. Ideally, BPD would be recognized at a young age and scaffolding constructed so that by adulthood the borderline would be on healthier and safer ground. Unfortunately, this is rarely the case for several reasons, including the derelict duty of pediatricians to consider psychiatric issues, teachers do not have clinical training, many borderlines do not show obvious symptoms of the disorder until late adolescence or young adulthood, and many parents remain idealistic or optimistic, hoping the child will simply grow out of what is deemed a difficult stage of development. If you need trustworthy scaffolding get a dog.

Get a Dog (But Only One)

The average dog is a nicer person than the average person.
- Andy Rooney

A dog doesn't care if you're rich or poor, educated or illiterate, clever or dull. Give him your heart and he will give you his.
- John Grogan, *Marley and Me*

There are many advantages in puppets. They never argue. They have no crude views about art. They have no private lives.
- Oscar Wilde

Sleep next to someone you love even if he has four legs (not to be confused with a throuple). Never minimize the value of external validation from a dog or being surrounded by positive and happy stimuli. We love dogs and they love us unconditionally without judgment or criticism. That we have to venture to another species to gain love and self-understanding cannot be more bizarre. (God did just that, and pursued man to understand affect). Dogs are blank slates, unconcerned if you are rich or poor, thin or fat, and they certainly don't care if you're a borderline. Dogs are the ultimate transitional object and constant object all rolled up into one. *Dogs absorb whatever feelings we project onto them and they reflect back whatever fantasies we have about how they love us unconditionally.*

Dogs also assist with the most fundamental issues for borderlines—trust and loyalty. The trust and loyalty that exists between the borderline and his dog is a perfect match for many reasons, including the fact that the dog has only one owner, the dog is dependent in a healthy way on the owner, and the dog shows repeated appropriate and expected appreciation for his food, shelter, toys, and playtime. The dog may even feel greater devotion to the borderline because of his neediness.

Every time a dog's head is patted, it reacts in a very similar way. When you interact with or say something to a human, the human will react with varied behavior or words, which causes the borderline uncertainty and anxiety. But the dog has very few basic and predictable responses, which provides the borderline certainty and calm. Borderlines often have difficulty with self-expression, yet dogs need no explanation at all and naturally tune into the borderline's needs, moods, and even personality type simply by being a companion. Dogs are also extremely malleable and can be trained to act and respond in various ways so that the dog can match the behavior, emotion, and thinking of the borderline. Finally, dogs have no sense of time so it doesn't matter how long you're away because when you reconnect it's as if time stood still and they are waiting, tail wagging for hugs and kisses. Dogs are amazing companions and sometimes what the borderline needs more than anything else is simply a nonjudgmental companion.

The best part about having a dog is that it can serve multiple purposes in the home for multiple people. For example, you may think that your dog is the most intelligent and beautiful dog in the world while your girlfriend reluctantly puts up with the smelly hound, confounded by the dog's compulsion to lick his privates, because you live in a sketchy neighborhood and your girlfriend thinks the dog makes the home safer. People (and girlfriends) come and go, but the lovable dog is a constant and therapeutic ally in a way few other things ever will be. Friends can't be easily replaced but you can replace a dog about every twelve years depending on the breed and the new dog will quickly tune into your habits and moods, allowing the borderline to reboot.

What about cats? I think dogs, particularly large dogs, have a better capacity for emotional soothing and companionship than cats, especially because dogs can be taken into the community as a companion, serving as a way to meet people and start conversations. Additionally, there is a visceral and affective response from dogs that seems less evident with cats perhaps because dogs actually smile while cats hiss, at least to me.

Reconsider Reproducing

Your children are not there to support your emotional needs. You are there to support their needs.

– Rabbi Shais Taub

It is forbidden to put a heavy yoke on your children and to be exacting about expecting the honor. So that you should not cause the child to stumble.

– Maimonides, Kibud Av V'em 6:8

I've put so much effort trying to find someone who is miserable like me that I don't even try to find someone who is happy. I can't imagine what a happy person would want with me.

– Anonymous

Genetics plays an overwhelmingly important role in who and what we are. Borderlines need to be aware that all genes are passed down and influence behavior, emotions, and thinking. If the borderline hates living with BPD and has sometimes thought about what it would be like if he was never born, he should consider not having children and sparing them from BPD. The borderline tends to be a terrible parent because he does not have the emotional capacity to soothe his own needs let alone the needs of another needy and demanding person. In fact, one of the reasons that two borderlines struggle to create a successful, healthy relationship together is because each borderline cannot attend to his own personal needs nor to the needs of the other, resulting in simultaneous interpersonal dysfunction.

The borderline may feel intimidated and even threatened by the positive attention given to his child which the borderline never received growing up. Borderline parents tend to project feelings of inadequacy onto their children even more so than on partners and friends. The first child tends to get the worst of it, but it's not a picnic for the other children either. Because the borderline has such a poor sense of self and probably low self-esteem, the borderline will nitpick about the child's behavior, thoughts, and feelings in a rigid and even hateful way. The borderline will become so enmeshed with the child that the borderline will be unable to provide competent parenting skills or even respect appropriate boundaries. It is also common for the borderline parent to idealize one child providing him unlimited support and yet demonize another child, withholding care, love, and support so that the child feels isolated emotionally and physically. Some children who have borderline parents find that they become parentified children, essentially adopting adult caretaker roles that require executive functioning and responsibility in order to maintain the home and the family. This is similar to children who grow up in a home with an alcoholic parent or even a parent who suffers from a chronic medical disease where the child must act as an adult and assume responsibilities far beyond what is considered developmentally appropriate. *If you cannot take care of yourself, how can you possibly expect to care for a child who, by definition, is constantly needy and unformed?*

Choose Someone Who Can Tolerate You

People think I hate myself. That's not true. I love myself. It's everyone else I can't stand.
    – Anonymous

The proper basis for marriage is a mutual misunderstanding.
    – Oscar Wilde

> Codependency is basically a maladaptive coping mechanism when
> living with a borderline. It's illness based attachment.
> - Anonymous

There's a myth that borderlines must remain single because they cannot tolerate long-term relationships, as they become emotionally intense and physically overwhelming. The second myth is that no one could tolerate a borderline in a committed relationship. Both are false. Many borderlines both enjoy and benefit from long-term relationships, greatly improving the quality of their lives. *The borderline must partner with someone who does not become offended or psychologically overwhelmed by the borderline's affect, interpersonal control and manipulation, or crazy thinking.* Such people are often docile and deferential and fall into two broad categories without overgeneralizing—schizoids and obsessionals.

Schizoids proactively avoid social interaction and have a limited range of emotional expression. Most importantly, schizoids cannot fully cognitively or emotionally process the borderline's emotionality so that the borderline's dysfunction does not register with the schizoid. It's as if the borderline's emotional dysfunction is blue and because the schizoid is colorblind to the color blue, it has no real meaning to him. In contrast, the obsessional is a person who is so preoccupied with his own thoughts and personal anxieties that he does not have the energy or capacity to become overwhelmed by the borderline's issues and so again the borderline's issues do not fully register with the obsessional partner. The schizoid in particular is often viewed as a loner and may indeed lack a desire to form close interpersonal connections in part because of his limited range of emotional expression. The schizoid or obsessional partner may also have limited interest in sexual relationships, which is crucial because intimacy can be overwhelming for the borderline. The schizoid may even perceive that he cannot experience pleasure, which of course is not true; it is only that his sense of pleasure or what he can experience may be more narrow or particular as compared to other people. Schizoids may have difficulty expressing emotion, may seem humorless, and may have limited motivation, seemingly indifferent to praise or criticism. This is also crucial because the borderline may project his low self-worth onto his partner and only the schizoid can tolerate such vitriol. The schizoid has a lifelong condition so that the borderline, who gains a successful relationship with a schizoid, may indeed find a life partner. Paradoxically, sometimes the schizoid's emotional lacunae causes the borderline to feel misunderstood and frustrated, as evidenced by the schizoid being unresponsive to the borderline's emotionality. The schizoid's emotional lacunae and the obsessional's detachment may also confirm the borderline's unconscious core belief that the world is a cold and uncaring place. Ultimately, there are personality types who can provide the borderline solace and love, care and instrumental support, and understating and tolerance, providing that the borderline considers the road less traveled.

Consider the Road Less Traveled

George Costanza: Why did it turn out like this for me? I had so much promise. I was always personable, I was bright. Oh, maybe not academically speaking, but I was perceptive. I always know when someone is uncomfortable at a party. It became very clear to me sitting out there today that every decision I've ever made in my entire life has been wrong. My life is the opposite of everything I want to be. Every instinct I have in every area of life, be it something to wear or something to eat. It's all been wrong.

Jerry Seinfeld: If every instinct you have is wrong, then the opposite would have to be right.
     – *Seinfeld*, S5:E22

> The purpose of [taking a walk in nature] is to evolve the way we
> see the world when we're not engaged in these acts.
>> – Rick Rubin

> Not all those who wander are lost.
>> – JRR Tolkien

Many people—including health experts—will tell you that in time things will improve and that your healthy instincts will steer you in the right direction. Yet, for some borderlines, problems remain the same or even worsen. Don't assume that things are going to improve or that you have the capacity to help yourself. This may sound horribly pessimistic, but if the borderline has made an earnest effort to seek professional help to make positive changes and nothing is working, then consider abandoning therapeutic strategies and long-term planning in favor of momentary satisfaction and adopting a less conventional pathway. This is particularly important for the borderline who becomes isolated, phobic, socially withdrawn, and unable to derive enjoyment in his everyday life. Living without enjoyment is not living at all and when that happens, experimenting with different choices and lifestyles may be a viable alternative. *True change and innovation depend on discovering unlikely outcomes, not predictable ones.* The tried and true avenues may be very different from what the borderline needs. Obviously, this is potentially perilous for borderlines who engage in self-destructive sexual or other impulsive behaviors that are inherently dangerous, yet when nothing else works, trying the opposite—the road less traveled—may be surprisingly helpful. In the words of Robert Frost:

> *I shall be telling this with a sigh*
> *Somewhere ages and ages hence*
> *Two roads diverged in a wood, and I—*
> *I took the one less traveled by*
> *And that has made all the difference.*

Don't Leave the Movie Early

Boris: Sonja, are you scared of dying?
Sonja: Scared is the wrong word. I'm frightened of it.
Boris: That's an interesting distinction.
    – Woody Allen, *Love and Death*

I tell Diane who has a mortal fear of death that there is nothing to worry about. Because if you have ever had a colonoscopy they give an injection and you're out and it's black and peaceful and nice. And so death is like a colonoscopy. The problem is that life is the like the prep day.
    – Woody Allen, speech at Diane Keaton AFI Award

Any idiot can face a crisis. It's day to day living that wears you out.
    – Anton Chekhov

Death is basically a very deep anesthetic where all sensation is stopped, so that anybody who's had surgery should not fear death. It's painless. I had the unique experience (or perhaps not so unique experience) of being contacted by the dead and we also had a ghost in our home. One weekend we rented a cabin in the Poconos. In the middle of the night I had a dream where a woman with long hair surrounded by total darkness was trying to communicate with me. I ignored the dream when I woke up the next morning. A few minutes later an old friend called to say that a woman I had known died the night before. There is no question that it was this woman. We had no contact for many years, though we had a special relationship and clearly she was trying to contact me immediately after her death. Since I'm at it, I'll share another true ghost story.

It began when I noticed that after we came home lights in the bathroom were on. I'm a stickler for turning out all the lights in the apartment when leaving and, being a bad husband,

I would often ask (accuse) my wife if she left the lights on and she would insist that she did not (though her memory is admittedly awful). We also had a dog who would bark wildly, staring at the ceiling, clearly indicating something was there even though I couldn't see anything. When we moved to our new apartment the ghost followed us. The same thing happened. We would turn off the lights in the apartment when we left and when we returned the lights were on. And then on several occasions, I saw an orb of light move across the kitchen floor. Initially I thought it was a mouse but no one in the building had mice, we never saw mice, and so I plugged up every hole. One day in our new apartment our dog began to bark wildly at the bathroom sink as if someone were standing there, which he never did before, and suddenly someone (or something) smashed the bathroom vanity. I won't tell the end of the story, though I have had other experiences. Fearing death is just a massive waste of emotional energy.

At the end of Mel Brooks' *Blazing Saddles*, there is a surreal ending where the good guys and bad guys from the Old West find themselves on their own movie set fighting it out. The hero kills the evildoer and the movie is essentially over. However, the hero insists on entering the movie theater where *Blazing Saddles* is playing. When his friend asks why, the hero replies "to see how it all turns out." Life is a little like that. There may be value in sticking around just to find out how it all turns out and the ending might just surprise you. Besides, borderlines make terrible ghosts.

Keep Your Sense of Humor

I don't think I have unreasonably high standards, but when the show is billed as a comedy I expect it to be funny.
– TV Guide Editor

The disarming power of laughter allows viewers, for the moment at least, to overcome their fear and find the truth amidst dishonesty.

> – Joshua Garroway and Wendy Zierler, *These Truths We Hold*

Voluntarily expose yourself in measured doses to what you're afraid of. You're always afraid except when you learn not to be. You unlearn terror. Learn to tolerate fears. People discover that they are bigger than their fears, though their fears are not trivial.

> – Jordan Peterson

A joke works because there's a paradox that the listener is not expecting and it forces the listener to confront the discrepancy. Life is a joke and not even a cosmic joke. There is probably no plan, everything is ephemeral, and it's possible that even reality doesn't exist. With this perspective in mind, nothing really matters and even morality is suspect. We hang out with a few friends, go to school, make some trouble, and yet we never expect that by early adulthood we'll be so fucked up (or conversely, successful). Almost all borderlines can point to real or perceived trauma in childhood, but it still doesn't prepare them for the reality of life's challenges. I'm not suggesting that the BPD diagnosis is a joke or not real, but that BPD just gobsmacks the person in the face. It can be helpful to maintain your sense of humor and reconceptualize everything as just one big joke, putting into perspective the diagnosis, which can otherwise assume a larger-than-life role and overpower the individual. And so with this in mind I will tell my father's favorite joke, which should preferably be read in a Yiddish accent.

MAY I HOLD YOUR TESTICLES?

Mrs. Goldberg, a fragile, elderly Jewish lady, is a new customer at Manhattan First National Bank. Every week she comes in and deposits about $5,000. The bank manager, Mr. Wasp, is very impressed by this new customer and wants to meet her in person. Finally, Mrs. Goldberg comes in one day and makes an even more substantial deposit, and Mr. Wasp invites her into his office. Mr. Wasp says, "I'm very pleased to meet you, Mrs. Goldberg, you have become a preferred customer at our bank with your large deposits. May I ask what kind of work you do?"

Mrs. Goldberg replies, "I am a gambler."

Mr. Wasp says, "That must be a very risky line of business because you win and you lose."

Mrs. Goldberg replies, "It's not risky for me because I never lose."

Mr. Wasp says, "You realize that's impossible. I now feel a little bit uncomfortable allowing you to place large deposits in our bank under the circumstances."

Mrs. Goldberg says, "I think I can prove to you that I am telling the truth."

"How?" asks Mr. Wasp.

"I will bet you $5,000 that next week I will come into the bank and your testicles will be gone."

Mr. Wasp is stunned. He says, "I can never take that bet because we both know that it's impossible and we both know I will be taking your money improperly."

Mrs. Goldberg says, "If you really feel uncomfortable then I am sure there are many other banks in the city that would be happy to take my money for deposits."

Mr. Wasp is very concerned for his position at the bank and so accepts Mrs. Goldberg's bet. Mr. Wasp says, "Just so we are legally clear, we are betting $5,000 that in one week you will come back to the bank and my testicles will be gone, is that correct?"

"Yes, that is correct," says Mrs. Goldberg. "No more testicles."

Mrs. Goldberg and Mr. Wasp politely shake hands and she

leaves the office. As she does so, Mr. Wasp has a concerned look on his face and discreetly touches his pants.

The following week, Mrs. Goldberg enters Manhattan First National Bank, but this time she's with a friend, Mrs. Cohen. They wait patiently outside until Mr. Wasp invites Mrs. Goldberg into his office.

"May I bring in my friend, Mrs. Cohen?" asks Mrs. Goldberg.

"I think for this particular situation privacy is probably important," says Mr. Wasp.

Mrs. Goldberg says, "Please understand that I need someone to verify whether or not your testicles have vanished."

Mr. Wasp says, "Well, obviously my testicles are still there. You're obviously going to lose the bet."

Mrs. Goldberg says, "It's important that someone verify all of my bets otherwise I cannot continue."

So Mr. Wasp allows both Mrs. Goldberg and Mrs. Cohen to enter his office. Mr. Wasp shuts the door for privacy and says, "I don't know what to say, obviously my testicles are still on me so you owe me $5,000."

Mrs. Goldberg says, "You must take off your pants and your underwear so I can look at your testicles."

Mr. Wasp says, "That's absolutely ridiculous, obviously they're there."

Mrs. Goldberg says, "Unless you show me proof, you must pay me $5,000 as we agreed."

Very reluctantly, Mr. Wasp loosens his belt, drops his pants, and then his underwear. "See! My testicles are still there," says Mr. Wasp with exasperation, standing with his testicles exposed.

Mrs. Goldberg says, "I don't believe you, I think those are fake."

Mr. Wasp say, "This is ridiculous. What more proof do you want?"

Mrs. Goldberg says, "I need to hold your testicles in my

hand and feel them so that I know for myself that they are real."

"This is outrageous," says Mr. Wasp, "obviously they're real."

"Without holding your testicles in my hands I'm afraid you must pay me $5,000."

"Fine," says Mr. Wasp.

And with that Mrs. Goldberg goes over and grasps the bank manager's testicles with her hands, feeling them, weighing them, fondling them, and inspecting them until she is satisfied.

"So finally," says Mr. Wasp, "you owe me $5,000 and you have lost your first bet!"

"To the contrary," says Mrs. Goldberg. "I bet you $5,000 that your testicles would be gone but I bet Mrs. Cohen $10,000 that the bank manager of Manhattan First National Bank would drop his pants, underwear, and allow me to hold his testicles in my hands. So I will be depositing $5,000 today."

Almost No One Will Understand You

You cannot make everyone feel and think as deeply as you do. That is the tragedy. Because you understand them but they do not understand you.

– Daniel Saint

There is no guarantee of justice except the personality of the judge.

– Eugen Ehrlich

I have a niche specialty and I don't think there's another person in the United States who does quite what I do. I've repeatedly explained my work, including to some colleagues and friends, and even some of them just don't get it. We want people to understand us. We want people to understand our behavior, emotion, and thinking, including our idiosyncrasies and proclivities. However, when a person has an unusual or even unique problem, it's understandably very hard for other people to feel empathy. This is especially true for BPD, where there is a cluster of symptoms that comprise the disorder, making it very difficult for anyone to understand the choices and inner life of the borderline. In fact, even mental health professionals are sometimes stymied to understand idiosyncratic behavior, emotion, and thinking—and psychopathology. Therefore, *just as the borderline must be compassionate and patient with himself, he must be equally compassionate and patient, always keeping in mind that most people simply cannot understand his personal issues and challenges, including perhaps even his life partner.* For example, explaining why self-cutting provides psychological and even physical benefits is quite difficult to articulate. Similarly, a cancer patient and his family rarely understand the complexity of the medical issues, but rather only a rough outline because without medical training the pathogenesis and pathophysiology of the cancer is almost in-comprehensible. Thus, if you really want to maintain friends and family, get it into your head that most people really can't (or won't) get you. Understanding BPD is not only intellectually difficult, but emotionally exhausting. *You should hope for meaningful connections with other people who can understand and identify with the most positive and wonderful aspects of who you are.*

Mirror Staring

After trauma, reacquaint yourself with your body.
    – Bessel van der Kolk

You are the only audience that matters.
    – Rick Rubin

> Better not to think too much. Rely more on the body—the body
> is more dependable. It shows up for meetings and looks good in
> a sports jacket.
> – Woody Allen, *The Condemned*

> Moving, be like water. Still, be like a mirror. Respond like an echo.
> – Bruce Lee

The capacity to self-soothe is the ability to find mechanisms or strategies to quell internal anxiety before it spills out into the external world and interpersonal relationships. Self-soothing allows the borderline to be less dependent on unhealthy relationships or unhealthy external supports which often provide only temporary relief and may even reinforce the borderline's sense of helplessness. Self-soothing often starts with physical self-acceptance.

For most people, looking into a mirror provides immediate superficial feedback about appearance. Borderlines may consider looking into a mirror in the same way that someone holds a yoga pose. When you go into a yoga pose it's not the stretch that matters but the calm breathing and relaxation—the new normal—when holding the pose and contorting the body in a new way. Similarly, the borderline should look in a mirror without any hope of an immediate answer but just stare, relax, breathe, and consider the possibility of a new normal—and a heightened sense of awareness may follow. Often the borderline does not feel comfortable with his identity or image such that it's crucial for the borderline to accept who he is not just emotionally and cognitively but physically—unconditionally. The feedback from the mirror is immediate, honest, and yet blissfully silent without judgment. Stare and relax. Just sit there. Be patient and see yourself in a way that you have never seen yourself before, and self-acceptance will slowly emerge. *Tolerate the image in the mirror without judgment and in time the image in the mirror will tolerate you—because it is you—and positive self-regard will emerge, decreasing over-all stress and anxiety.*

Eating Healthy is Not a Panacea Nor is Exercise

Eat to live. Do not live to eat.
 – Moliere

Wine and tobacco destroy the individuality. After a cigar or a glass of vodka you're no longer Peter Sorin, but Peter plus somebody else. Your ego breaks in two and you begin to think of yourself in the third person.
 – Anton Chekhov, *The Seagull*

Food has become a panacea for all medical ailments. I have a genetic/medical issue and, no matter how healthy I eat, it will not disappear. Similarly, countless children and adults have suffered through various food elimination programs for medical and psychiatric issues with little or no success. However, eating healthy allows for a strong physiological system even staving off genetic issues, which is imperative for people who have chronic medical and physical illness and which helps minimize body and brain inflammation, especially from dangerous sugars, among other toxins. (It would seem that cold water also helps reduce inflammation and may even help reset the endocrine system). There are innumerable websites about healthy eating and I will only summarize my food preferences.

- Herbs – no, not those kinds (parsley, dill, oregano, basil, mint)
- Mushrooms – no, not those kinds (a wide variety)

- Spices – turmeric, cumin, cinnamon, ginger

- Berries – blackberries and blueberries

- Leafy greens – kale and spinach (and cabbage and seaweed)

- Fish – salmon and sardines

- Cruciferous/non-starchy vegetables – broccoli, cauliflower, brussels sprouts

- Fruit – apples, pears, figs, dates, apricots, prunes

- Olive oil – follow the Mediterranean diet

- Superfoods – non-pasteurized honey, egg, garlic, onion, radish, tabouli, quinoa, avocado, yogurt, bok choy, herbal teas, beets

- Zero cigarettes, drugs, or alcohol – sorry, but none is best

Just as healthy eating is not a panacea, exercise is also not a panacea for BPD or other disorders, though research suggests that regular cardio and weight exercise allows for improved physical and mental health and self-control. Although some clients have noted the benefits of massage therapy, a lesser-known option is machines that squeeze the body, providing surprisingly effective psychological and physical support and almost immediate relief from anxiety and stress. People with Autism Spectrum Disorder especially benefit from such machines. *Exercise and diet are important because, as a rule, serious mental illness is accompanied by generalized physiological changes and those changes tend to have a net negative effect on the body.*

External Security Permits Internal Control

To everything that I have ever lost. Thank you for setting me free.
- Faraway, Instagram

Quiet is Un-American.
- *Get Smart*, S3: E22

Because the borderline's internal world can be chaotic, it is essential to have external stable, secure, and safe parameters in the form of personal, home, or community supports. Internal chaos can be balanced against external predictability, allowing for the borderline to enjoy certainty which is crucial to psychological and emotional comfort. Additionally, BPD can be a noisy disorder so that external security will mute the internal noise. Sometimes blocking out reality is necessary to cover up the truth of existence, allowing for moments of contentment to be strung together like a popcorn necklace. As the borderline's mind is already sufficiently cluttered, a healthy home and clean environment are crucial. *Just like the borderline should discard unhealthy relationships, useless or burdensome objects within the home that detract from calm should likewise be discarded.* For borderlines, simplicity and quiet is key.

Listen, Look, and Learn

God is silent. Now if we can only get man to shut up.
- Woody Allen

When you're at a loss for words, the trick is to stop talking.
- Robert L. Bartley

If you cannot control what you put in your mouth at least try to control what comes out of your mouth.
- Anonymous

For borderlines, knowledge comes from listening and asking questions, as constant inquiry is needed to clarify meaning due to cognitive distortions and social anxiety. *The borderline's emotional dysregulation and impulsive rush to judgment prohibits the normal risk-benefit calculation of a situation, made even more uncertain because the borderline's first instinct is often negative, partly due to hypersensitivity and guardedness.* Similarly, a person with autism must learn to interpret and understand (decode) verbal and nonverbal communication, as a means to successfully navigate his environment and those people in it. (Almost everyone can distinguish between a smiling face and a sad face, but what's interesting is that some people interpret a neutral expression as simply neutral while others interpret it as disappointment). It's important to suspend judgment about other people's thoughts and feelings—and even facial expressions—before truly understanding what the person is trying to convey. Just as oratory is a lost art so is listening. Listen carefully, say very little, ask relevant questions, do not upset the listener, and listen for what is said and also not said. In general, checking impulsivity requires a proactive approach to stave off unintended behavior and speech. In particular, before speaking, consider very carefully your thoughts, how you want to phrase your words, and who you are speaking with. There is an old Jewish adage: "A word is worth one coin and silence is worth two." It was my grandfather's favorite saying.

The best phrases to use to interact in a non-confrontational way are:

- I wonder...

- Perhaps...

- Could it be that...

- If I understand you correctly...

Someone who begins with these phrases or uses them during conversation will be less likely to be attacked given the passive language and reflective nature of the inquiry. If in doubt remain silent and don't interrupt. Take a few moments to reorganize or reconsider your thoughts or questions. Consider the possibility that you are asking questions in the wrong way, poorly phrased, or that they are irrelevant or questions that will not properly elicit meaningful material from the other person. Silence allows the other person to consider his thoughts without outside noise or distraction.

In general, when we become acutely anxious we may also become overly focused on the object that induced us to feel nervous or unsafe. This tends to cut off peripheral vision which, in turn, adds to anxiety. When this occurs look around, take a sip of water, stretch the body and head, and literally shake off the feeling.

Empathy can be demonstrated by verbal expressions of understanding or even a nod or smile. If the other person feels heard he will respond with gratitude with emotional involvement and greater honesty, and thus more willing to consider further interaction. With empathy, the person will perceive that he is understood, appreciated, and will believe that what he is saying is validated simply by the other person's empathy. This technique is used in clinical therapy to develop a therapeutic alliance with the patient at which point the conversation can be limitless because once the patient feels trust, a trove of information will follow.

The large majority of communication is meta-communication, that is, non-verbal communication that we may be totally unaware of. Master communicators monitor their bodies as much as their words, because both convey messages—benign and serious. Body language can also stave off anxiety or nerves through preemptive movements. Body language can also be used to mimic empathy, or it can reflect immediacy and importance. Calm body language can be soothing while physical agitation can be negatively infectious.

Body language can be used aggressively against someone

but also to help calm another person. I enjoy taking notes at an angle, partly because of a right shoulder limitation, but primarily because it allows me to speak directly to the client face-to-face and also pivot to the side for note-taking, so the client does not feel that he has to look at me every second as if under an interrogation light.

While most miscommunication issues with borderlines are interpersonal, borderlines also have difficulty communicating with themselves, that is, their internal voice may not be clear or coherent. Just as the borderline should listen and look before responding, he should also consider his own internal narrative with patience and love. Internal narratives can be explored by talking through issues out loud or in autobiographical writing describing behavior, emotion, and thinking. (Generally, autobiographical writing is superior to journals because while journals are linear reflecting day-to-day thoughts autobiographical writing tends to be edited allowing for greater flection and in-depth thinking). If you wish to write about yourself then do so with total honesty. The draw- back is that people fear that their writing will be seen (and judged) by others, causing them to feel horrible shame when, in fact, writing should inspire.

Make It a Habit to Be Inspired

People do not decide their futures. They decide their habits and their habits decide their future.

– F.M. Alexander

Make it a habit to habituate healthy habits.

– Anonymous

Make it a daily habit to be inspired by the opposite of you and expect to be inspired—and start somewhere. Try to gain momentum as you craft a plan today so that tomorrow won't just be an experiment but a healthy and positive routine. Focus, release your anger, and share the very best of who you are. You need no other audience and you don't need to drive yourself crazy searching for the perfect path. Allow your supports to emerge from your natural needs, and amazing gifts and good habits will follow. There is nothing wrong with external validation but structure your day, environment, career, and friends and be your own civil engineer. Borderlines do better with prescribed parameters of behavior, though discipline does not limit freedom; it expands it. Be your own collaborator. The reason that hard work is healthy is because it distracts from destructive behaviors and reinforces positive habits. We get what we expect, so expect the best from your habits and planning. Until you change your behavior you will always recycle your thinking. Until you change your thinking you will always recycle your behavior. Although self-exposure can lead to vulnerability, without self-exposure life would be undeveloped. *Safety is important but dull is deadly.*

Refresh your mind, clear your problems away, and just have fun with life. Don't complain. Enjoy life! Recapture your childhood curiosity and mischievousness. Troublemakers are cool. Progress, no matter how modest, goes in the win column. Don't compare yourself to others; compare yourself to the progress that you have made, giving yourself credit for learning how to be normal by evaluating situations and engaging with the world in a safe and healthy way. You are not a disappointment. You are who you are and your pathway is your own.

Choices make us happy, though too many make us unhappy. Keep stress low but not too low. Eliminate risk and gain certainty in healthy habits. Challenge yourself with brain teasers, Tetris, books, and athletics. When you take responsibility for yourself, you not only stop blaming others for your problems but you also give yourself credit for your accomplishments. Do things that do not come naturally to you, but are natural for most people. Your chaos is bound by rules and assumptions. Test them or move past them, but don't remain bound by what doesn't make sense. Use your strengths, identify what to change, take baby steps if needed, but conquer your fear and progress will occur. Don't personalize or absorb criticism. *No one would judge you as harshly as you judge yourself.* Start every day with a clean slate. Decode what is around you to make sense of the world to gain freedom, including financial freedom.

Financial Independence is Priceless

There was no damned romance in our poverty.
   – Eugene O'Neill, *Long Day's Journey into Night*

I love liberty, and I loathe constraint, dependence, and all their kindred annoyances. As long as my purse contains money it secures my independence, and exempts me from the trouble of seeking other money, a trouble of which I have always had a perfect horror; and the dread of seeing the end of my independence, makes me proportionately unwilling to part with my money. The money that we possess is the instrument of liberty, that which we lack and strive to obtain is the instrument of slavery.
   –Jean-Jacques Rousseau, *Confessions*

Never underestimate the value of financial independence (often achieved through professional career advancement) as a means to attain personal security as a foundation to enjoy life. However, for low-functioning borderlines, properly accessing social service support from both nonprofit agencies and government programs can be crucially important to enjoying a good quality of life.

Volunteer to Help Others in Need

Mental illness makes you feel that you're the center of the world because your issues are overpowering and consume mental energy. And yet, you're not that important.
- Anonymous

No matter how you feel, get up, get dressed, and show up.
- Regina Brett

Give of yourself and you won't be any less of yourself, only more. Through selfless compassion for others, it's possible to grow in a way that may be unavailable even with the best clinical therapy for borderlines or anyone.

CHAPTER 6

Conclusion: Authenticity

The goal should not be the pursuit of happiness, but the happiness of pursuit.
> – *Hector and the Search for Happiness*

Do silly things. Foolishness is a great deal more vital and healthy than straining and striving after a meaningful life.
> – Anton Chekhov

It does not matter how the facts occur in life. It matters how they are told.
> – Elsa Morante

Authenticity means repairing perceived injuries allowing for self-cohesion and healthy ego-functioning without suffering guilt, shame, or self-recrimination for things that you are not responsible for. Remove unhelpful idealizations and anxiety-ridden panic about external judgment in favor of realistic and mature images, yet without sacrificing hopes and dreams. *Authenticity is achieved not by connecting but by reconnecting with you and your family or partner in a genuine way without jealousy or anger while acknowledging that flaws are inherently human and yet not barriers to contentment or fulfillment.* Re-own ambiguity that causes disappointment with humor and humility.

The good life is not devoid of disappointment, failures, and struggles. *The good life is assessing disappointments, failures, and struggles and not deifying them.* There are two essential secrets to life. Life is a matter of priorities and life is about missed opportunities. Prioritize your needs and personal values allowing for authenticity. Stop stressing over things you can't control or change and tackle matters right in front of you. Develop strategies and even daily planning focusing on what you love, not what makes you anxious.

Leaving the fault of everyone else aside, ask: What role do I play in my problems? What role can I play in helping myself? What role can I play in healing others without harming me?

Allow the brain to process information for at least a minute before considering what behavior, emotion, and thinking means. Don't interrupt when listening. *Teach the brain to disconnect from daily life and to not anticipate.*

Allow love to heal unconditionally, suspending your disbelief about the realities of life. Cherish loyalty in friendships because they may be few and far between. Don't strive to be loved by others; just improve yourself. When hurt by others, allow time for emotional recovery just as you allow your body to recover from physical injury. Take a chance and say hi to a stranger. Fairweather friends are fine, but one positive friend can make all the difference (even if he has four legs). Be appreciative of those who are helpful. Embrace rejection as a gift, allowing freedom from destructive relationships. Your support can come from anywhere and in any form and at any time. Don't assume that you know what works for you even if it seems intuitive.

You have value as a human being and personal dignity is priceless. Don't give others the benefit of the doubt; give yourself the benefit of the doubt, quelling boredom and the internal critical voice (from others who demean you). Besides, people are much more forgiving and understanding than you might imagine. Never allow parts of you to be torn away because a divided self cannot function. We have enough martyrs. Don't self-sabotage and become a self-fulfilling prophecy of doom and don't romanticize being screwed up. There's nothing wonderful about it. Take ownership of your behavior, emotion, and thinking, be your own prophet of hope, and create your own life. Stop taking responsibility for things that you're not responsible for. The question is not how do I learn to love myself, but why in the world would I hate myself? *Choose what is hard—always favor meaning over meaningless—and conquer what you choose.*

The perfect time does not exist and hope dies last. Happiness is a journey informed by connection and accomplishment. Scratch just under the surface and there is someone fragile and vulnerable, but also someone amazing, strong, and brave. Be strong and brave. There is time. There is a lot of time.

ABOUT ATMOSPHERE PRESS

Founded in 2015, Atmosphere Press was built on the principles of Honesty, Transparency, Professionalism, Kindness, and Making Your Book Awesome. As an ethical and author-friendly hybrid press, we stay true to that founding mission today.

If you're a reader, enter our giveaway for a free book here:

SCAN TO ENTER
BOOK GIVEAWAY

If you're a writer, submit your manuscript for consideration here:

SCAN TO SUBMIT
MANUSCRIPT

And always feel free to visit Atmosphere Press and our authors online at atmospherepress.com. See you there soon!

ABOUT THE AUTHOR

MARK S. SILVER is a New York State Licensed Clinical Social Worker (LCSW) and lawyer with a doctorate in psychology, masters in political science, and post-graduate certificate in family therapy. He is the author of several publications, including "Handbook of Mitigation in Criminal and Immigration Forensics: Humanizing the Client Towards a Better Legal Outcome" Seventh Edition (2021), "Psychosocial Evaluations and Consultation in Civil Litigation: Strategies to Understand and Humanize the Client" (2021), and two novels: *The Mystery of the Dead Dean: Res Ipsa Loquitor* (2018) and *The Arranged Marriage: My Kalpa* (2018).

He has lectured to thousands of lawyers throughout the United States on a wide range of forensic issues with case samples. His primary focus is showing how psychosocial evaluations can assist lawyers to better understand the client's clinical issues, allowing for more informed legal advocacy. Since 2002, he has worked as a consultant for many law firms throughout the United States conducting psychosocial evaluations and writing formal forensic and mitigation reports in criminal, immigration, and personal injury cases. He has worked with clients from over 50 countries on various individual, family, and mental health issues. He has been qualified to provide expert testimony for numerous cases in Federal Immigration Court.

www.ingramcontent.com/pod-product-compliance
Lightning Source LLC
Chambersburg PA
CBHW021537150726
47990CB00006B/2281